carlos raúl villanueva

MASTERS OF LATIN AMERICAN ARCHITECTURE SERIES
An international joint project developed by Birkhäuser – Publishers for Architecture, Logos Art, Princeton Architectural Press, and Tanais Ediciones. Part of the Biblioteca Iberoamericana de Arquitectura collection, BIENAL IBEROAMERICANA DE ARQUITECTURA E INGENIERÍA CIVIL Ministerio de Fomento del Reino de España, Junta de Andalucía.

carlos raúl

villanueva

Paulina Villanueva
Maciá Pintó

Photographs by
Paolo Gasparini et al.

Princeton Architectural Press, New York

carlos raúl villanueva

First published in English
in North America in 2000 by
Princeton Architectural Press
37 East Seventh Street
New York, NY 10003

For a catalog of books published by Princeton Architectural Press, call
toll free 800.722.6657 or visit www.papress.com.

First published in Spanish by
Tanais Ediciones, Madrid—Raúl Rispa, Publisher
Guillermo Vázquez Consuegra, Series Director
Erica Witschey, English Editor

Original drawings: Carlos Raúl Villanueva/Fundación Villanueva,
Alexander Calder / Fundación Villanueva
Texts: Paulina Villanueva (essay), Maciá Pinto (selected works),
Fundación Villanueva and Tanais Editorial Team (biography and
chronology), Juan Moreno, Fundación Villanueva and Tanais Editorial
Team (bibiography)
Plans: Roberto Sosa with Mateo Pintó and María Antonia Rodríguez,
Fundación Villanueva. The University Campus illustrations form
part of the "Proyecto Ciudad Universitaria de Caracas. Patrimonio"
exhibition coordinated by Ana María Marín, FAU, UCV
Photographs: Paolo Gasparini *et al.* (see page 180)
Documentation: Fundación Villanueva
English translation: Gavin Powell
Copy editor: Cathryn Drake

Design and layout: Tanais Editorial Team
Electronic Edition: Natalia Billotti
Layout of Selected Works: Mercedes H. Marrero
Cover design: Sara Stemen and Deb Wood

Special thanks to: Ann Alter, Amanda Atkins, Eugenia Bell, Jan
Cigliano, Jane Garvie, Caroline Green, Beth Harrison, Mia Ihara, Clare
Jacobson, Leslie Ann Kent, Mark Lamster, Anne Nitschke, Lottchen
Shivers, Jennifer Thompson, and Deb Wood of Princeton Architectural
Press—Kevin C. Lippert, Publisher

Printed in Spain

Library of Congress Cataloging-in-Publication data for this title is
available from the publisher.

ISBN 1-56898-204-6

Carlos Raúl Villanueva is one of the great figures of twentieth-century architecture. If he had been European, North American, or Japanese, rather than Venezuelan, he would be known today all over the world. Highly considered by the most respectable critics and historians, his work appears in architectural treatises (including those of Benevolo, Curtis, Frampton, and Pevsner) and large millennium exhibitions organized to act as an epilog to the century. Like so many of his Latin American colleagues, he built at a time when the industrialized world was killing and destroying itself—during World War II and the Cold War—and when the conscience and the voice of a Third World were emerging. He worked far removed from those media circles that today publish and disseminate anything, no matter how inane, as long as its image "works." For these reasons, Guillermo Vázquez Consuegra came up with the idea of making a book about this very special man, who had not had a book brought out about his work since 1964, when Sibyl Moholy-Nagy, an university professor teaching in New York, published hers. At that time, some of the greatest of Villanueva's works had still not been produced.

This seminal proposal soon turned into a more far-reaching scheme: to document and publish on an international scale the *Masters of Latin American Architecture*, a concept that, combined with a project that was being considered at that time by Dr. Rucki in Basle, has given rise to the first volume of the series that is being published simultaneously in English, German, Italian, and Spanish.

This work has been made possible thanks to the cooperation and contribution of a number of people and institutions. First, by the generosity of the *maestro's* daughter, the architect Paulina Villanueva, former dean and professor of the School of Architecture and Town Planning at the Central University of Venezuela, which was cofounded and designed by her father, Carlos Raúl, and which has for many years zealously guarded his documentary legacy. Second, thanks to the Regional Council of Andalusia and its Directorate General for Architecture, headed by Víctor Pérez Escolano, whose unstinting work made possible the research that was necessary to study an architect whose complete work had, to date, never been inventoried. The immensity of this task can be judged by the fact that no less than 135 of his works are included here. So many other people were involved in putting together this book that it is impossible to express thanks to all of them individually. Among those who merit special note are the architects Maciá Pintó, for his meticulous work, and Enrique Larrañaga, for his insight.

This is the first volume in the Ibero-American Library of Architecture and Town Planning, a series of publications aimed at accompanying the Ibero-American Biennial of Architecture and Civil Engineering, a courageous project backed by the vision and sense of duty to the discipline, art, and profession of architecture demonstrated by the Subdirectorate General for Architecture of the Ministry of Public Works of the Kingdom of Spain and its director, the architect Gerardo Mingo Pinacho.

All merit for this work goes to these people. Any defects are the fault of the publishers.

Raúl Rispa

Carlos Raul Villanueva

Carlos Raúl Villanueva, Architect

Paulina Villanueva

Carlos Raúl Villanueva lived and breathed architecture. The people who knew him, including his closest relatives, found it absolutely impossible to separate the man from the architect. In his letters and personal documents, he had the habit of reaffirming this indissoluble union by referring to himself simply as "The Architect."

Until Carlos Raúl's generation, there had been no tradition of architectural practice in the Villanueva family. His paternal grandfather was a surgeon whose strong interests in politics and history led him to a public life, including posts as the provisional president of the Venezuelan republic and rector of the Central University of Venezuela. Carlos Raúl's father studied engineering at the Paris School of Mining but never practiced the profession, following instead a diplomatic career in France, Belgium, Germany, Spain, and England, where he served as the Venezuelan consul general between 1896 and 1900. Like his father, he was an amateur historian, interested particularly in the liberation of South America. As it turned out, it was Villanueva's older brother, Marcel, who introduced Carlos Raúl to the world of architecture. Marcel studied in Héraud's studio at the Ecole des Beaux Arts in Paris, and Carlos Raúl followed in his footsteps. Although they came from the same background and received the same training, the two brothers could not have followed more different paths. Marcel settled in the United States—returning to Venezuela on only a handful of occasions—and produced conventional architecture following the patterns prevailing in North America at the time. In stark contrast, Carlos Raúl set off in search of new forms of expression and an encounter with the history of Venezuela, a young country brimming with opportunities and a fertile ground for his personal vision.

Villanueva's training at the Ecole des Beaux Arts was to become the solid foundation on which he would erect all of his work. Beyond the thematic trivializations and stylistic strictures it imposed, the school provided extensive historical training while preparing him in the craft of design, shaping his mind, his eye, and his hand—the three essential tools in the practice of architecture. To think in an orderly manner in accordance with logical and rational principles, to see through to the essence of things, to clearly understand the problems and the relationships that exist between buildings and the contexts in which they are situated, to master all the scales of design, and to make of the built work a source of knowledge—these were the keys to his education. In essence, the school gave him rigorous preparation in the fundamental principles of architectural composition, the key component in the physical realization of an architectural idea and an essential instrument for the conception of form.

The school educated his eye and his hand, the one inseparable from the other. He learned to rationalize his experience in an active and ordered way—in notes, drawings, magazine and press cuttings that he carefully classified by theme—to truly see the world and thereby acquire a greater sensitivity, to appraise as well as to measure. He was challenged to elevate his drawings to complete levels of expression, and to use them not only as means of representation but as tools to shape his personal vision. Villanueva was a fine draftsman: he had an idiosyncratic way of sketching, in which he used strong yet precise strokes that enabled him to compose complex ideas with few lines. When working, he would make innumerable small sketches to achieve a preliminary design that he would return to again and again, constantly modifying and altering it throughout the life of the project. This process of revision and change would have been interminable had it not been for the need at some moment to decide on a concrete form for the work.

Villanueva never attached any value to his drawings beyond the utilitarian role they served in the creation of a particular project. Indeed, he placed so little value on his prodigious graphic output that he simply threw most of his drawings away, dumping them into the wastepaper baskets of the various organizations for which he worked. All that was left once a building was finished were the project plans, few of which were actually drawn by Villanueva himself. However, it was also his habit to continue drawing a project after it was finished, and some of these sketches have been conserved. Also remaining are the handsome notational drawings that he reproduced in colored chalk on blackboards during his classes on the history of architecture. These drawings are also vividly preserved in the memories of his students.

The method of work fostered in the studios of the Ecole des Beaux Arts is also important in considering Villanueva's later career. It was there that he learned to work on a team and to collaborate in the design of a common project. In one case, for example, when he was unable to compete alone because of his status as a foreign student, Villanueva teamed up with fellow student Roger-Leopold Hummel to produce a design that won the Prix de Rome. These experiences proved to be invaluable after he returned to Venezuela, where he often participated on teams of professionals for various state organizations.

Villanueva designed and built without pause, accepting and overcoming the hypocrisies inherent in the architectural profession and in the country in which he chose to practice it. Seeing himself as a man of action rather than words, he identified with the French architect Auguste Perret, with whom he maintained a strong friendship and who had a profound influence on his work and ideas. With Perret he shared the driving need to build and the profound conviction that architecture is the art of organizing space. For Villanueva, the making of architecture was an activity for which he knew no limits. The sheer volume of his built work attests to this voracious desire. He was a relentless designer, working countless hours on both his most important commissions—those that earned him a place in the history of twentieth-century design—and also on the smaller, more anonymous projects that have faded from memory.

In 1928, once he had completed his studies and acquired some work experience in France and the United States, Villanueva settled permanently in Venezuela. There, under the dictatorship of Juan Vicente Gómez, he began his professional career as an architect working for the Ministry of Public Works, a department for which he would carry out significant work throughout his life. His first jobs were executed in the city of Maracay, which was the seat of central power at that time. In those days

Jesús Soto's *Cajita Villanueva*, 1955

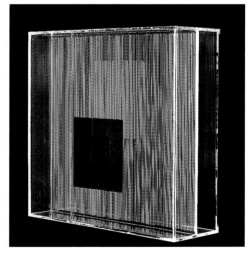

Villanueva with students at his studio in 1961

Venezuela was a poor country with little notion of what architects did; before Villanueva's return it had been the engineer that had been dominant in the field of public works. He thus began an anonymous series of works—renovations, designs of plazas and houses for the Gómez family—until he received his first important assignment: the Hotel Jardín in Maracay (1929–30). This commission entailed the transformation of a residential building, facing what would be the Plaza Bolívar, on which work had already started and which had originally been designed by the French engineer André Potel. The result exhibits some of the elements that would become standard features of Villanueva's architecture: covered galleries used for protection from the weather, the articulation of different volumes within a whole, and interior courtyards and gardens deployed to create a harmonic interplay of built and unbuilt spaces.

During this early period in his career, Villanueva discovered and suffered the vicissitudes of Venezuelan politics, a politics prone to improvisations, last-minute changes of plan, impossible deadlines, pre-established inauguration dates, and fast-track construction initiated without set designs. He nevertheless remained, despite all obstacles, a committed professional guided by the deeply rooted idea that architecture is a social action. This noble belief explains why Villanueva worked primarily for the state. By day, he accepted the conditions imposed on him by Venezuela's difficult cultural and political environment. But at night, after his work was complete, he would read to colleagues from the books he had brought with him from Paris, including the writings of Le Corbusier, whose call for a new architecture he had made his own.

However, it was Villanueva's first private commission which marked his presence as an architect on the Venezuelan scene and enabled him to put to the test what he had learned in his years in Paris. The Maestranza—or bullring—in Maracay (1931–32), like all of his early academic designs, was executed in line with the tastes of Venezuelan society at the time, with a functional typology that was predetermined, and it was constructed within the limitations imposed by the nation's unskilled workforce. Though this commission cemented Villanueva's professional standing, it was only after Gómez's death and the launching of Villanueva's career in Caracas that he truly began to plot a new course for himself as an architect.

The construction of a private house in La Florida in 1934 offered the architect his first chance to build in the language of the modern movement. The house was indeed radical—so much so that it failed to satisfy the programmatic requirements of a family residence and the environmental demands made by its site and the local climate. Here Villanueva learned a hard lesson about dogmatism, and, without abandoning his firm adherence to the principles of modernism, began to follow a path that enabled him to explore a variety of design themes that he would develop in his later, better-known works.

Villanueva's ideas about housing and its effect on the practice of everyday Venezuelan family life matured through a series of jobs executed between 1933 and 1938 with his father-in-law, Juan

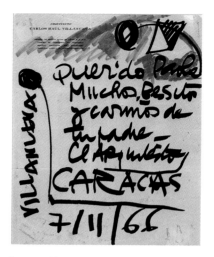

Letter to his daughter Paulina

Bernardo Arismendi, one of the driving forces in the development of Caracas. These commissions were for small, rapidly executed speculative houses that, because of their number and variety, gave the architect considerable room for experimentation and proved a significant influence on his later housing projects for the Banco Obrero.

At the same time, the little-known work he carried out for the Ministry of Public Works brought him closer to the themes that would propel his later work. This was particularly true in the case of the numerous hospitals he designed, such as the Tuberculosis Clinic in Mérida (1942–45) and the prototype hospitals for the country's interior (1938–40). These provided Villanueva with crucial experience in this typology, which he would call upon in the design of the hospital at the University Campus of Caracas (1945–54), one of his most significant projects. With each of these projects Villanueva explored the themes established in his earlier work in Maracay: the articulation of different bodies within a work built in stages; the use of covered corridors and galleries as basic components from which to structure the whole; the insertion of courtyards with interior gardens to establish a relationship between interior and exterior spaces; and the organization of volumes around a central plaza. Another theme developed in the hospital was the application of a fenestration system that incorporated—through the use of lattices and canopies—the wisdom of traditional Venezuelan design. Complemented by the building's corridors and garden patios, and by the incorporation of additional openings to permit the free passage of breezes, this system ensured pleasant temperatures and cross ventilation—crucial in the Venezuelan climate.

Two other works dating from this period should be highlighted: Buena Vista Boarding School in Los Teques (1940–42) and the National Leper Hospital in Los Caracas (1944, later transformed into a resort). Although these complexes differed in function, they were both designed as urban agglomerations: cities on smaller scales. Villanueva's goal was to make them autonomous communities comprised of groups of buildings with different functions, just as in a traditional urban fabric. Indeed, these two projects were Villanueva's initial attempts at urban design. There were separate facilities for housing, education, leisure, and services. The ideas explored in these designs would eventually be carried over into his most significant urban plan: the design and layout of the University of Caracas, a monumental project on which he labored for the three decades from 1940 to 1970. There is, of course, a difference in scale, meaning, and architectural value among these works, but it is interesting to note the persistence of certain design themes throughout Villanueva's oeuvre.

Between 1935 and 1938 Villanueva designed and built his first major work in Caracas: the Museum of Fine Arts, at the entrance to Los Caobos Park. The simplicity of the museum's initial layout was driven by the fact that work on the building was commenced before there was even a preliminary program for it (in an effort to provide jobs for workers at the end of the Gómez dictatorship and the beginning of General López Contreras's government). Villanueva was an appropriate choice for the

Sketch of Caoma and Sotavento, 11 x 15,9 cm, unsigned, 1958

commission, given his interest in the arts. This sensitivity and devotion —which had been cultivated from his natural sympathy for the modern movement—was demonstrated in his extensive library, in which books and publications on art competed with those on architecture. It was also made apparent by a stroll through the private worlds he created for himself in the houses in which he lived. These were invariably filled with works from the artistic vanguards of the century, a testimony to his intimate friendships with a good number of the world's leading artists.

Not surprisingly, museums and exhibition pavilions occupy a prominent place in his oeuvre. Moreover, from his early experience in the Museum of Fine Arts, a clear line of reinterpretations of the same theme can be drawn: in the possible analogies between the first museums in Caracas and the Venezuelan Pavilion designed for the Paris Exposition of 1937; in the contrasts between the first building (1952) and the second extension (1968) to the Museum of Fine Arts or the late design for the Jesús Soto Museum in Ciudad Bolívar (1970); or in the unique nature of the Venezuelan Pavilion for the Montreal Expo (1967); until arriving at what would indirectly be his largest museum and the most public one of them all: the University of Caracas (1952). It is important to note that his involvement with museums extended beyond his designs for them; throughout his life he was an active participant in Venezuela's cultural life, organizing exhibitions, acquiring works, and promoting artists.

The idea of creating a synthesis among the arts was one of the principles that marked all of his work. In the commission for the Museum of Fine Arts, he worked with the Venezuelan sculptor Francisco Narváez, with whom he had already collaborated in 1934 in the construction of the Plaza Carabobo in Caracas. Narváez also worked with Villanueva on a series of later commissions: the Natural Science Museum (1936–39), the Gran Colombia School (1939–42), the Rafael Urdaneta Plaza (1945), and the University of Caracas.

In 1937 Villanueva returned to France to supervise work on the Venezuelan Pavilion for the Paris Exposition Internationale des Arts et des Techniques Appliqués à la Vie Moderne, a project situated on the delicate threshold between art and architecture. His attendance at the fair turned out to be extremely significant, for it placed him at the epicenter of the contemporary debates on architecture and art. After numerous setbacks and controversial architectural competitions, the fair finally took place with the participation of many leading figures in the architectural community, among them Alvar Aalto, Le Corbusier, Robert Mallet-Stevens, the Perret brothers, and José Luis Sert. The exhibition was a promenade of architectural objects of varying design but, more importantly, delved into the theme of the indissoluble relationship between art and technology to show that there was no incompatibility between beauty and functionality. Numerous artists took part in the exhibition, including Alexander Calder, Robert and Sonia Delaunay, Henri Laurens, Fernand Léger, Joan Miró, and Pablo Picasso, producing sculptures, bas-reliefs, and large frescoes. This experience exerted a deep influence on Villanueva, who maintained friendships with many of the architects and artists he met at the fair. Several of these artists, in fact, would participate in his "Synthesis of the Arts" project, developed during the construction of the University of Caracas.

This project, which also extended to his works beyond the walls of the university, took shape as the different buildings on the campus came to fruition, maturing along with his architecture. One example from beyond the university setting is the polychromatic decoration of the large blocks of housing built for the Banco Obrero in the late forties and fifties. But a more ambitious path was explored at the university when the project was carried forward by a number of Venezuelan artists who produced murals, sculptures, and even a decorated ceiling (by the artist Narváez for the university canteen) at the various university buildings. Two sculptures and a fresco by Narváez were included in the first buildings of the School of Medicine, in 1945. The primary volume of the University Hospital, completed after a long interruption in work, was animated by the use of vivid colors applied by Mateo Manaure, who was also responsible for several murals in the hospital and a large relief decorating the façade of the workshop of Villanueva's Industrial Technical High School (1948).

Villanueva's design of the Central Area of the University Campus of Caracas (1952–53) marked a new stage in the architect's conscious integration of art and architecture; his layout was made up of five routes—like five movements in a symphony—that fostered a dialog that continues to stimulate members of the university community as they make their daily rounds. Here, sculptures by Jean Arp, Henri Laurens, and Antoine Pevsner, along with murals by Armando Barrios, Fernand Léger, Mateo Manaure, Pascual Navarro, Victor Vasarély, and Oswaldo Vigas comprise what is merely a preamble to two of the most spectacular works of the "Synthesis of the Arts": the mobiles created by Alexander Calder for the interior of Aula Magna Hall and the large stained-glass window designed by Fernand Léger for the entrance hall of the Central Library (both of 1952–53). Clouds of color and shafts of light opened up a path of unlimited possibilities with which to redefine the relationship between architecture, art, and nature in a way previously unequalled.

It was Calder, during his first and only visit to Venezuela—in 1955, two years after the completion of Aula Magna Hall—who gave Villanueva his nickname: The Devil. As far as Calder was concerned, only a demon could have carried out such a mischievous work as Aula Magna. As a testament of his profound and sincere admiration and as a token of his deep friendship for the architect, Calder executed a sculpture he titled *The Devil´s Chair* (1955), which remains standing in the garden of the Villanueva house in Caoma.

During the last stage of construction of the campus, comprising building work on several schools, Villanueva continued to deck the interiors with works of art that increasingly blended with the architecture—in the broken rhythm of walls, behind the surfaces of perforated screens, by the ramps, under the wells of light—always emphasizing the kaleidoscopic nature of space. Wifredo Lam's mural relief for the Botanical Institute (1948) stands out among these, as do the works executed by Jean Arp and Sophie Taeuber-Arp for the School of Humanities (1953–55), the pieces designed by Alexander

Pic-nic assembly designed by Villanueva in 1966

Villanueva at his beach house in 1961

Calder and Jésus Soto for the School of Architecture (1954–56), and various murals and stained-glass windows conceived by Miguel Arroyo, Alirio Oramas, Alejandro Otero, Braulio Salazar, and Víctor Valera. Beyond these individual works, the force of Villanueva's synthesis of art and architecture was carried by the polychromy of his buildings' façades, their dynamic rhythms and contrasts of color and texture, and the richness and plasticity of their forms—all of which served to create an architectural environment that was essentially inhabitable sculpture. The University Campus of Caracas can thus be understood as a living museum in which art is inseparable from architecture, and in which art becomes a companion to daily life.

In addition to its integration of art and architecture, the University Campus of Caracas should be viewed as one of the most exceptional and successful examples of modern urban planning and development. For Villanueva, town planning and architecture were always two sides of the same coin. When he returned to Paris in 1937 to supervise the construction of Venezuela's entry in the World's Fair, he decided to stay on for a few months to take a course in urban planning. A few years later, he won a competition to carry out the redevelopment of El Silencio, one of the worst slum districts in Caracas. Completed during the early forties, this remains one of Villanueva's most significant legacies.

El Silencio marked the beginning of an extended period of experimentation in the field of low-income housing and planned residential development. Between 1941 and 1957 Villanueva worked, without significant interruption, on a series of housing projects for the Banco Obrero. His participation in this vast building campaign entailed the design of housing prototypes and the building of entire block-size housing cooperatives. It was a project that allowed him to realize one of the grand dreams of the modern movement: innovation in the field of housing within the broader concept of urban planning.

In addition to El Silencio, between 1945 and 1949 Villanueva designed the San Martín Cooperative Housing Unit in Caracas, a development of four housing blocks with more than three hundred apartments. Though similar in its architectural vocabulary to El Silencio, San Martín—a far smaller development—provided different challenges in terms of plan. During this same period Villanueva also produced his most important public housing work in the interior of the country: the General Urdaneta Neighborhood Unit in Maracaibo (1943–47). This massive development—it accommodated a population of 7,300—featured several design innovations, including curving streets, separation between automotive and pedestrian traffic, and the use of central thoroughfares as key elements of the layout. The design of the individual buildings of the development echoed the vernacular architecture of the region, incorporating various formal elements that would subsequently recur in Villanueva's later housing projects: projecting eaves, mobile wood shutters, and openings in the façades and interior walls that enabled air to circulate freely and imbued the works with a feeling of transparency. (These design themes found more complete expression in the housing Villanueva

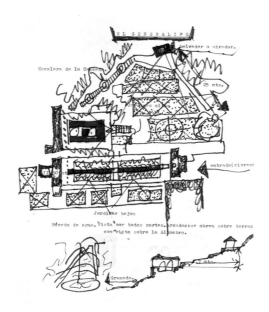

Villanueva's notational drawings for his classes on the history of architecture

designed in Los Caracas in 1944.) The development's CT1 apartment block is worthy of specific mention. In this unit, Villanueva treated the exterior stairways as precise volumes deployed to break up the monotony of the wall surface. In the years following the design of the General Urdaneta development, Villanueva continued to use stairwells and circulatory corridors as forceful visual elements that animated his designs.

In 1948 Villanueva began work on two projects of exceptional importance for the city of Caracas: the Francisco de Miranda and the Coronel Delgado Chalbaud housing projects. These developments were designed with a new formal language. (This language resurfaced in his unbuilt design for a residential unit in the Rental Zone of the University Campus, which in turn became the inspiration for the student residences Villanueva designed at the university in 1949.)

Villanueva's participation in the large-scale urban development of the city of Caracas culminated with the El Paraíso and 23 de Enero developments (1952–54 and 1955–57, respectively). These massive projects—virtual cities within the city, providing housing for thousands—combined high-rise "superblocks" based on Le Corbusier's Unité d'Habitation model with low-lying wings. The fall of the Pérez Jiménez dictatorship in 1958 brought an end to Villanueva's nearly twenty-year period of experimentation in the field of public housing, though the many developments he created remain standing.

Beyond his design work, Villanueva played an active role in Banco Obrero's architectural studio (known as TABO), a center from which new ideas on architecture were disseminated throughout the country. Architects, artists, and students met at the studio, which sponsored exhibitions, conferences, and publications within a progressive intellectual environment where architecture was understood as a tool for social betterment and urban transformation.

Not surprisingly, given his own role in the development of Caracas and other Venezuelan cities, the history of the Hispano-American city and of Venezuelan colonial and popular architecture grew into an object of Villanueva's constant attention. In 1950 he published Caracas of Yesterday and of Today, a testament to the simple wisdom of Venezuelan vernacular building, with a special focus on how indigenous builders had adapted to the country's climatic conditions. Villanueva embraced elements of this vernacular tradition in his own work, seeing them through the lens of modernism and thereby creating a fertile dialog between old and new. Despite his European training, Villanueva found his roots within the Venezuelan tradition.

Villanueva's masterwork is without question the campus and buildings for the University Campus of Caracas—indeed, the rest of his projects can be seen as preparation for it—a massive undertaking both in terms of urban planning and architectural design. During the course of more than twenty-five years, beginning with his first Beaux Arts–inspired plan of 1944, Villanueva personally supervised the project. He worked under the aegis of the University Campus Institute, which directed planning and execution of the project until 1958, and then under the Office of University Planning

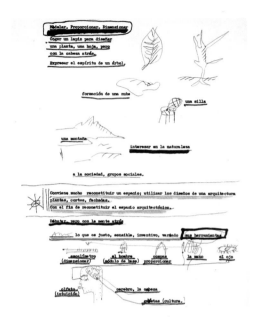

Villanueva's notational drawings for his lectures on architecture

until the late 1960s, when his health forced him to leave the project and the university with some of the buildings still in the design stage. This vast urban complex, comprising 220 hectares of land (roughly 90 acres) and a total of 40 buildings, demanded all of his experience as an architect and town planner. As an urban unit, the University Campus remains one of the most successful applications of modernist planning in Latin America. Though conceived from whole cloth by a single man, it can be understood as a living, ever-changing organism subject to continuous transformation.

The only part of Villanueva's initial scheme of 1944 to be completed was the medical area, with buildings for the Schools of Medicine (1945), Nursing (1946), and the University Hospital (1945). The Industrial Technical High School (1948) was also built according to the early plan, housing in its extensive and varied body classrooms, workshops, laboratories, dormitories, an auditorium, a cafeteria, and sports facilities. The buildings of the high school were endowed with an autonomy that announced the functional complexity of the individual schools and the faculties they would support in the future. This feature is worthy of note, since it gave rise to the development of an interesting relationship between the whole and its parts, designed as individual units within an all-encompassing framework.

In the second stage, the buildings for cafeteria services (1949–50), student residences (1949), and the School of Engineering (1950) were completed, each group with its own formal logic. Two stadiums (the Olympic Stadium and the Baseball Park, both of 1949–50) were built at the same time, positioned at the opposite end of the campus from the hospital, creating a central axis.

The 1952–53 project for the Central Area of the campus marked a significant transformation in the preliminary scheme, which gave way to a more differentiated organization that, though ordered, repudiated the symmetry of the earlier design in favor of one that was more dynamic, innovative and functional. Villanueva's drive to search and innovate linked him to other *chercheurs,* in his own words, and led him to execute designs in which past, present, and future came together in a single discourse. Devoted to the ideology of his time, Villanueva conferred special value to the flow of traffic within the campus. The roads were ordered and structured from the focal point of the three gateways to the campus, and were linked to a system of open parking lots that served the buildings and were considered valued parts of the urban complex: vehicles were understood as necessary rather than hostile elements. Pedestrian circulation, however, was treated independently. The pathways of Villanueva's earlier residential schemes and the galleries he created for the redevelopment of El Silencio were synthesized at the university, where covered walkways served as pedestrian streets that blurred the distinction between interior and exterior space and, through minimal transitions, allowed the university community to negotiate the spaces between the various faculties and schools. By blending the system of covered streets with generous ground-floor spaces, the architect created a single spatial unit with an edgeless quality that continues to stimulate daily life on the campus.

Alexander Calder's wire portrait of Villanueva

Serving the functions traditionally reserved for urban plazas, the ground floors of the campus's buildings were conceived as meeting places rather than mere entrances; places where the university's community life could flourish. These open spaces featured patios and internal gardens in which the intense tropical light was sifted and fragmented by perforated screens and pergolas. Cuts in the ceilings offered glimpses of the sky and silhouettes of the mountains, making explicit the relationship between the building, the campus, and the environment.

The heart of this urban space was the central Covered Plaza, an innovative space with a geometry that broke with the regularity of traditional plazas and a concrete canopy that provided protection from the climate—coverage generally offered by treetops in tropical climates. The most important buildings of the campus and the most significant works from the "Synthesis of the Arts" project were assembled around this bravura space, a masterstroke of urban planning in which Villanueva went beyond the frontiers of the traditional to give expression to the original.

Villanueva placed equal, if not greater, priority on the commodious design of interior space—the space where man and architecture interact—, which he considered to be the driving force behind any architectural work. His interiors have a solidity that is both physical and ethereal. They are utilitarian, but possess a beauty rooted in proportion and an architectural language rich in its application of light, texture, material, color, transparency, and reflection. They are complex and active spaces that act as stages for the lives they enclose.

In Villanueva's architecture, the strength of cantilevered roofs, the formal expression of structural frames and functional volumes, the spaciousness of façades with their eaves and sun-protection elements, the large surfaces of tile or perforated block, and the transparent bodies of the stairways, all come together to define a new role for the building, which takes possession of a point in space that it makes its own. His architecture transcends its physical limits, ordering space on a broad scale and with great meaning within a modern conception of urban form.

It is impossible to appreciate Villanueva's architecture fully through the pages of a book or the photographs of a magazine. It is necessary to experience it firsthand—to move within it and see it from different angles, contrasted against the sky or silhouetted against the mountains—to understand it and love it as many of us do. His work gives shape and expression to a noble conception of the role of architecture and those who practice it. "Architecture is the imprint of life on its highest level," he wrote, "and the architect, by development and function, is an intellectual first and foremost. He must also be a technician, because only as a technician can he fulfill the dreams of the intellectual. If these dreams become exceptionally rich, poetic, and alive, he might also become an artist."

selected works

Caoma House

La Florida Residential Estate
Caracas, Federal District
1951–52
Villanueva residence

The Caoma residence is the house of an architect who, together with his family and artist friends—the latter represented by their works of art—inhabited a space endowed with a special sensibility that has withstood the test of time. Simple and bright, it accommodates human life naturally (unlike the first house he designed in 1934, the manifesto of an early, schematic, and insecure modernity). Caoma is representative of Villanueva's architecture and of architecture at its most transcendent. It is also a clear statement of the incessant search that inaugurated Villanueva's most productive period. Here the architect conjugated the values of tradition and modernity—traces of which are still fresh and identifiable—in a synthesis that started to crystallize in the space between ideas and completion. Blending lessons of the past with glimpses of the future, the architectural themes and elements present in Caoma's design gain true significance in the context of the particular climate and culture that would form the framework of Villanueva's life and work. The house is a clear example of his intuitive and rational ability to extract elements from what he called the "functionality" of colonial and popular architecture. The volumes and openings, contrasts of light and shadow, eaves, slatted shutters and lattices, areas of calm and half-light, entry hallway, and landscaped court all lie at the center of an architecture calculated and scaled by—and for—man.

Caoma is a container, a box of spaces. Its white mass incorporates empty spaces, such as the garage. This opens onto the service patio above, which itself opens to the sky. Also open to the sky is the terrace courtyard at the back of the house, below which lies the gallery leading to the garden. Made up of two floors and located between the street and garden in an east-west direction, the building is practically closed in on three sides, opening on the fourth to a fresco of exuberant light and color filtered by tropical vegetation.

The ground floor is accessed by an open space that acts as an entry hallway and light well with a double door, leading from the street. To one side of this hallway is the separate service area, which extends out toward the plant gallery, connected by a stairway to the upper patio. To the other side lies the main living area, which consists of a single living and dining room that is open from wall to wall and from floor to ceiling, with large glazed flush doors and sliding windows that bring the changing image of the garden into the house. On the upper floor, the landing accommodates a small lounge that leads to the bedroom and bathroom area. This space is partitioned and connected by a traditional corridor and several doors that mark the space with an uneven topology. The dark wood surfaces of this section of the house ensure a leisurely, muted itinerary for intimate family life.

Villanueva considered the patio to be one of architecture's ever-present, ever-youthful elements—one open to new interpretations. Caoma is the faithful expression of this philosophy, with the plant-filled patio of the traditional house as its heart and guiding spirit. Although it is physically outside, it is nevertheless integral to the life of the house and its inhabitants, part of the essential raw material of interior space. In this way, the house ceases to be simply an object for view from the outside and becomes also an eye that looks outward.

1 Sketch
2 Interior patio

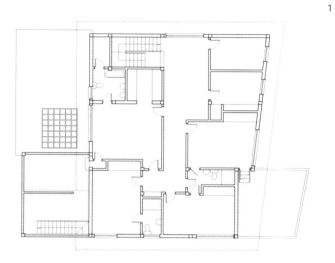

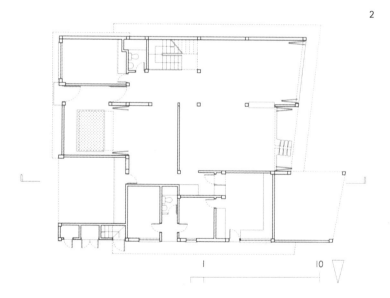

1　Upper floor

2　Ground floor

3　View of the sitting room from the staircase nucleus

4　Longitudinal section, through the garden

5　General floor plan

6　Detail of garden access and sliding-swinging door

4

5

2   10

6

1

2

1 Sketch of the house from the garden
2 View from the street
3 View of the garden from the sitting room

3

1

2

1 West façade from the garden
2 Detail of the shutters from the interior
3 View of the garden from the terrace
4 Detail of the outer enclosure
5 Villanueva in his studio

3

4

5

The Studio where Villanueva worked and spent time alone is in the garden, separate from the activity of the house. The long, narrow structure, built entirely out of wood in the shape of a railway carriage, has a bookcase with a line of high windows along one side. Along the other, a worktable runs the length of a wall directly under a line of latticed awning windows that open to the garden. At one end there is a door, and at the other there are three latticed doors and a small sitting area with an easy chair.

Just as in the *chambre de travail* annex to Le Corbusier's Cabanon de Cap-Martin, it is an intimate space. Like his sculptural constructions of wood, this structure, nestled within the garden, is a small architectural poem.

Sotavento House

Palmar Este Residential Estate
Carabellada, Vargas State
1957–58
The architect's beach house

1 South façade
2 View of the pergola gallery to the south

Together with the Gymnasium and the Swimming Pool Complex of the University Campus of Caracas, the Sotavento residence completes Villanueva's cycle of 1950s masterworks. A paradigm of his best architecture, this house anticipated by ten years the final synthesis embodied by the Venezuelan Pavilion for the Montreal Expo of 1967.

Sotavento is a light, transparent structure, a "window" house in the sense that it can be completely opened to the outside or closed to the inside. A small, well-proportioned construction, it is illuminated and animated as bright light and deep shadow move—atomized and fragmented—across the emptiness through louvers and lattices with the slow passing of the day.

Like many beach houses or weekend getaways, it has a spirit of total freedom. Located on the central coastal region of Venezuela, the Litoral Central, its architecture was designed for the sea breeze and dazzling light that characterize the works of Armando Reverón, a painter from Macuto. His paintings, alongside works of Wifredo Lam and Pascual Navarro, were an integral part of the house.

Sotavento stands on a small plot of land between adjoining houses, next to which it goes unnoticed, nestling as it does under a roof that is barely visible above the perimeter walls and dense vegetation. The two floors and two bodies that make it up—the public area and the bedrooms, on the one hand; and the service area with the kitchen behind, on the other—are situated in the garden, spreading fluidly over the entire plot of land. The house dissolves: it opens up to the morning sun with the bedrooms to the east; from there it continues, functionally and perceptively, to the north and south, in the front and back, with plant-covered galleries that extend the space to the boundaries of the land; it closes itself off to the west, where it leaves only a narrow chink between the wall and the roof for a line of light to filter in and sweep through the space at sunset.

Deceptively small from the outside, the spacious house is accessed alongside the blind west wall through a narrow passage that leads to a low space connecting the kitchen and the service area. From there one can get a full view of this single space, defined by the poured roof that descends on a continuous plane from the bedrooms on the upper floor, barely separated by a parapet.

Unlike the Caoma house, here the concrete structure is starkly emphasized through exposed beams and columns of varying dimensions. As in Caoma, they do not follow a predetermined grid or pattern; they simply stand where function dictated they should, fulfilling their structural raison d'etre. But perhaps the most characteristic features of the house are the prominent eaves, which go unnoticed in Caoma, and the walls and wood louvers painted white from floor to ceiling.

The whole house emanates an enveloping atmosphere, along with the pleasant sensation of being both in and out, overriding the limits represented by walls in architecture. The architectural historian Sibyl Moholy-Nagy, a friend of the architect and author of a book on his work, called it an object of "personal magic," the manifestation of a rich inner life, where interior and exterior, man and house, are one and the same.

1

2

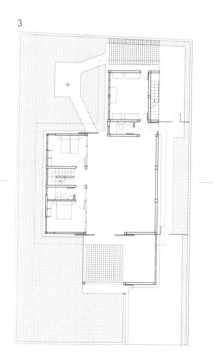

3

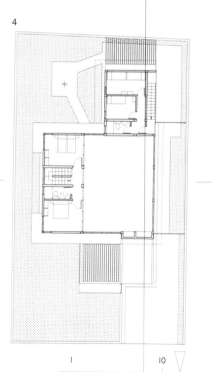

4

1   10

1 View of the staircase, a room, and the swimming
  pool from the sitting room
2 Sketch of the interior
3 Ground floor
4 Upper floor
5 Cross section through the staircase
6 View of the upper-floor rooms from the sitting room

5

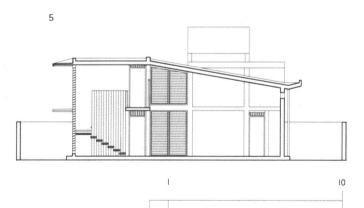

I   10

6

1 View of the double-height area of the sitting room
2 Sketch

El Silencio Redevelopment

Caracas, Federal District
1941–45
Developer: Banco Obrero

1 Sketch of the idea of the complex
2 Façade of block 1, looking onto Plaza Bolívar

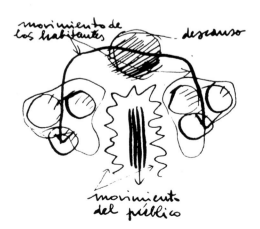

The redevelopment of El Silencio, one of the most insalubrious slums in the city at the time, was the first large-scale technical and engineering operation carried out by the construction industry in Caracas. More importantly, it was an unprecedented project of urban renewal and public housing. Significantly, the political-administrative complex originally designed by Maurice Rotival and laid down in the urban plans was never built; in its place, the Banco Obrero developed a new center for community life for a city in transition, consisting of public buildings around Plaza Bolívar and state housing encompassing seven city blocks. Destined to preserve the tradition of parishes, the new proposal of *unidades vecinales*, the traditional scheme of defined neighborhood units, was developed using the typology of the perimeter block with commercial galleries to the street and private courtyards to the interior. This model offered completely new solutions and related to both the morphology and topography of the city blocks and the position and orientation of the buildings. The public face of the complex featured a plaza and façades treated with an academic and traditional language; the private side consisted of courtyards and balconies expressed with a modern vocabulary.

Given the location and composition of the complex, this was deemed to be the best way of defining and formalizing a meeting place, a preexisting crossroads around the hill known as Cerro del Calvario, the dominant feature in low-lying colonial Caracas. It looked decidedly to the east, in the direction of the city's new growth, the starting point of the great avenue Avenida Bolívar, which ran along the axis of the valley alongside the River Guaire, as if it were the backbone of the city. From the opposite perspective, El Silencio represented a point of arrival on a truly urban scale, where the important development of Block 1, with the Cerro del Calvario in the background, forcefully rounded off the main plaza with the two fountains—whose dolphins were designed by the sculptor Francisco Narváez—that act as a center for the symmetry of the avenue's axis.

The public side of El Silencio—with its arcades housing commercial activity and animating life as well as serving as terminals for multiple public transport routes—is a space of much use and interchange. It is still a necessary reference point and an obligatory thoroughfare for movement through the city, despite the huge size of modern-day Caracas and the presence of other centers and poles of attraction. In the interior of the blocks, the loggias and balconies of the flats jut out over the collective courtyard, closing in an area whose scale gives rise to different relationships of visual and functional continuity. This implosion, together with the adaptation of the blocks to the curved or diagonal line of the streets and the rise and fall of the natural terrain, creates a dynamism and a surprising spaciousness in the interior courtyards not apparent from the outside.

El Silencio stands as a successful expression of a given city at a given time and a translation of a certain way of life as a result of its contextualization of public and private functions, its double language and symbolic value, its role as source of identity, and above all its stoic permanence. Indeed, in the face of aggression and deterioration in a constantly changing city, El Silencio remains one of the best and most valuable solutions to collective urban housing in a city center.

1

1 Area of redevelopment between Plaza Bolívar
(below) and El Calvario Park (above right)
2 Urban environment showing the new churches and
theaters built in Caracas at the time
3 Area of El Silencio prior to redevelopment
4 Floor plan of the ensemble
5 Detail of the colonnaded plaza

2

3

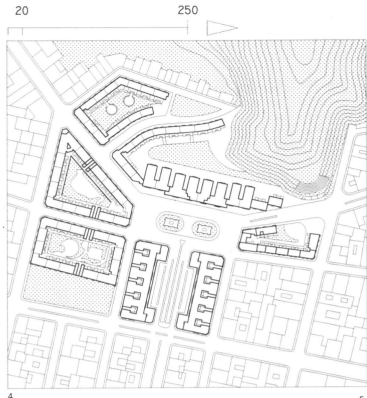

4

5

20   250

1

2

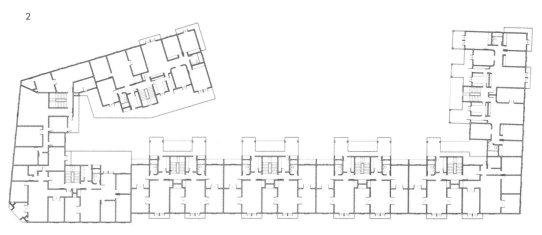

1 Courtyard behind block 1
2 Typical floor plan for block 4
3 Common courtyard façade

2   25

3

El Paraíso Development

Caracas, Federal District
1952–54
Collaborator: Carlos Celis Cepero
Developer: Banco Obrero

1 Plan of the complex
2 Main façade of block 1

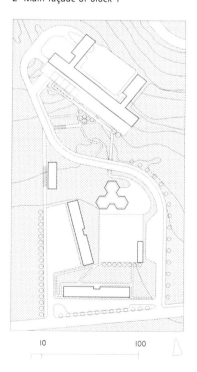

10   100

Within the framework of the National Housing Plan, a vast public housing program designed and executed by the Architectural Studio of the Banco Obrero (TABO) of which Villanueva was the chief architectural advisor, and together with the developments of Quinta Crespo (unbuilt) and Cerro Grande, the El Paraíso housing project is considered one of the soundest and most comprehensive housing solutions drawing on Le Corbusier's Unité d'Habitation models.

The initial scheme incorporated six buildings, of which only three were built: two smaller blocks and a large tower situated on the highest part of the land to offer better views and ensure satisfactory conditions of sunlight and ventilation. The "superblock"—a central body with two wings perpendicular to it—consists of building units that were combined and repeated to give shape to the whole. The bodies of the stairways and lifts define a vertical plane marked by concrete screens perforated with small openings; the circulation passages are protected by a continuous wall of concrete grills; and the structure forms a well-defined grid, further accentuated by the chromatic work of the Venezuelan artist Alejandro Otero. The most salient features of this polychromy are the "drawing" that uses the sides of the building to create a pattern of colors, playing with the inversion of the exposed beams above and below the roofs of alternating floors, and the dynamic effect achieved through the projections and diminishing sections of beams and columns as they rise up. The eighteen floors of the tower provide space for nearly two hundred split-level flats with two, three, or four bedrooms, commercial areas with some thirty shops and offices, two levels of parking, and communal facilities, including a library, a social club, a gymnasium, and a day nursery.

For Villanueva, society and the urban phenomenon were interdependent. In the redevelopment of El Silencio he articulated a community in the city center that would create a strong and lasting image. In the General Rafael Urdaneta Development, on what was then the outskirts of Maracaibo, he explored the indigenous models of popular housing in a rural environment to reinterpret them in an urban scheme of curved streets and pedestrian walkways with low houses that were either isolated or formed continuous rows between the densely planted gardens. In new proposals and models of modern urban housing, a major leap in scale made it possible to solve the problems and needs arising from new sanitary norms of communal life and collective education, using blocks that acted as huge containers of flats and communal facilities, the latter located in the lower levels of the buildings, as exemplified in another project, the 23 de Enero Development.

In El Paraíso, another residential group with a main tower including communal facilities, Villanueva's particular fusion of urban planning and architectural design is evident in a proposal for comprehensive community life within the architectural solution. For French architect Auguste Perret, the structural frame was the only legitimate adornment that architecture could possess. However, for contemporary urban planning this frame transcends aesthetic value to become an essential component of structured systems that house people. Likewise, in his urban proposals Villanueva used the typology of the block with exposed structural frames to create solid architectural images.

1 Upper floor of duplex apartments in block 1
2 Lower floor of duplex apartments in block 1
3 View of the lower blocks
4 Access to the service wing
5 View of the meeting between perpendicular bodies

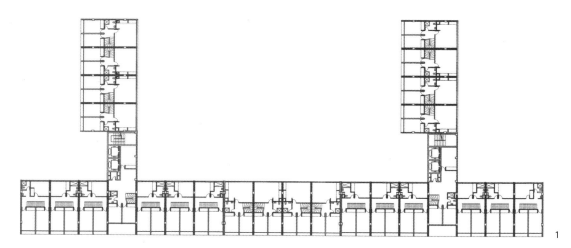

1

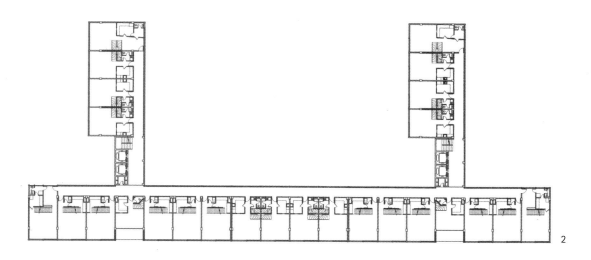

2

2   25

3

4

5

23 de Enero Development and Chapel of La Asunción

Caracas, Federal District
1955–57
Collaborators: Carlos Brando
José Manuel Mijares
José Hoffman
Developer: Banco Obrero

The 23 de Enero Development was the most important large housing project included in the National Housing Plan implemented in Caracas in the 1950s. A massive urban planning operation supported by the ideas and models of modern architecture, this plan was the forerunner of a social, political, and economic strategy that was implemented in a short lapse of time and on a scale probably unequaled to date in Latin America. The government's housing policy—aimed at transforming the physical environment and eradicating the city's shantytowns through large investments in public works—was channeled through TABO.

During the first phase of construction (1955, East Sector), 12 "superblocks," one of them a double tower, were built together with twenty-six four-level low-rise units, four kindergartens, four day nurseries, and four commercial buildings, adding to a total of 2,366 flats for approximately 15,000 residents. The second phase (1956, Central Sector) saw the construction of thirteen "superblocks," three of them double towers, together with nine eight-level medium-rise blocks, two primary schools, six kindergartens, four day nurseries, eleven commercial buildings, a market, and a civic center (with a church, cinema, and administrative building), adding to a total of 2,688 apartments for approximately 20,000 inhabitants. The last phase (1957, West Sector) added thirteen "superblocks," five of them triple and three of them double towers, seven four-level low-rise buildings, a triple unit and three double units, three primary schools, seven kindergartens, ten commercial buildings, a market, and a civic center for approximately 25,000 residents in 4,122 apartments.

Villanueva believed in the vast possibilities of the city for promoting culture and human contact, and subscribed to the ideas of contemporary urban planning, present in the directives drawn up by the National Urban Planning Committee (of which he was a member). He also believed in the vital role played by the circulation systems of a city, although he was convinced that they were not sufficient to create a true urban fabric. Likewise, he recognized the need to free the ground to introduce separate blocks with facilities whose orientation, lighting, and ventilation schemes ran along the lines sketched out in his teaching notes and classes on architectural history and planning. Under these precepts, the 23 de Enero Development became a self-contained city designed on large terraces following a basic scheme in which the different units were duplicated with variations and adaptations. This sometimes entailed excessive simplification, but was achieved with the mastery of large-scale design in which Villanueva was trained. The plan incorporated neighborhood units with commercial, educational, welfare, religious, and sports facilities. However, its fundamental feature was the housing block with split-level flats: a basic repeated unit that characterized the whole and that defined the urban profile.

Although Villanueva had already used less abstract approaches to contextualize the urban phenomenon, the 23 de Enero Development was important because it brought together a series of contradictions and problems that marked his development as an architect and town planner. But because Venezuela in the 1950s was a country in a social time lag, the early modern utopian values embodied by this gigantic experiment would have to be reexamined as they were applied in the mid-century.

Aerial view of the complex

1 Aerial view of the complex
2 Low blocks and service facilities
3 General plan of the complex

2

3

50   500

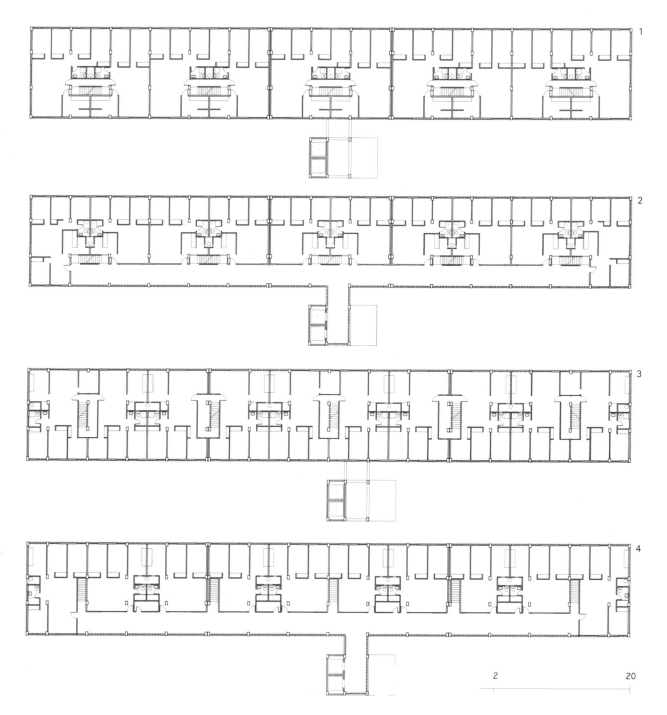

2   20

5

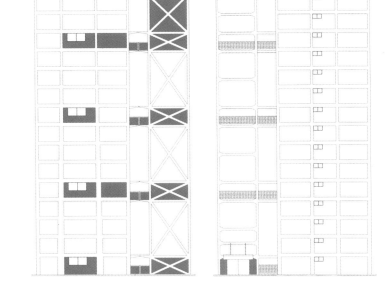

6

7

1 and 2 Block A, typical floor plans, duplex apartments

3 and 4 Block B, typical floor plans, duplex apartments

5 Exterior view of the superblocks

6 and 7 Side views of blocks A and B

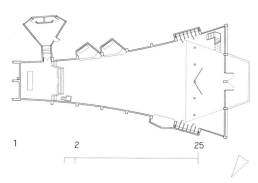

1 Ground floor plan
2 View of the inside from the main entrance
3 Main west façade
4 Sketch of the idea

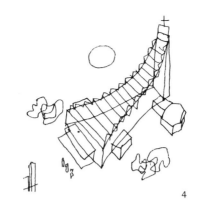

Chapel of La Asunción Among the different buildings of the estate, this small chapel, with its modest and dignified interior bathed in light, stands out for the contained strength of its outline, a zigzag that marks an ascending curve of spiritual elevation. The stark simplicity of the design is enhanced by the tension that arises between the two rough converging walls and the folded concrete roof. The double play of contrasts extends to the inside, where the wide and low space of the entrance gradually leads to one that is narrow and high. In keeping with the name of the chapel, "the ascent of the Virgin," the space rises in search of light as the luminous triangles of light that filter in through the ceiling get smaller and smaller, accentuating the effect on the wall behind the altar. Like some of its predecessors—the small colonial churches of Paraguaná and Margarita as well as the draft design for the University Chapel, which has the same folded roof aimed in a different direction—the Chapel of La Asunción is a pure, unaffected space, a burst of fresh air lifting and unfolding the roof toward the sky.

University Campus of Caracas (Ciudad Universitaria)

Caracas, Federal District
1944–70
Developer: Instituto de la Ciudad Universitaria

1 Model of the first design
2 Aerial view of the University Campus

Although it was executed with a large team of collaborators—mainly engineers and technicians, but also architects and draftsmen—the University Campus of Caracas was very much a personal achievement for Villanueva. Formed by nearly forty edifices built over three decades on 200 hectares, it is a monument to his constant commitment to architecture and was decreed a Venezuelan national landmark.

With an admirable capacity for driving the architectural process, Villanueva guided the specialists and artists involved in the execution of the design, both marking a firm direction and avoiding dogmas, fears, and prejudices—thus remaining open to changes and new requirements, boldly anticipating and experimenting with unprecedented solutions, testing and modifying the scheme in an unremitting search.

The first design was modeled on the American university campus, a self-contained area isolated from the city center, even though the site was the old Hacienda Ibarra, an area well connected to the new city center under construction around Plaza Venezuela. Like its American prototypes, the plan for the campus was derived from Beaux Arts traditions, with a symmetrical arrangement of buildings and open spaces along a central axis. The first phase of construction, including the University Hospital and the medical area, followed the lines of this plan. However, the new scheme, or rather the process that encompassed the remaining stages of construction, broke away from these hierarchies and followed a new layout incorporating modern ideas without excluding traditional features such as plazas and streets, courts and corridors, climate and vegetation, light and color. Together with the zoning of functional areas, the separation of motorized and pedestrian traffic, the expression of each tower or block in an isolated building, the identification of functions through specific volumes and shapes, and the use of an architectural language articulated through the structures and materials, these traditional values combined to turn a tropical conjunction of elements into a positive and polished whole.

Once the boundaries of the campus were marked—with the medical buildings to the west and the sports facilities to the east, the Botanical Gardens to the north and Los Ilustres avenue to the south—the interior became fertile ground for the design and building processes. Here, the central administrative-cultural area stands out as a unit, as do the towers and blocks of the schools, each unique despite a common typology and recurring elements used within variations—such as the open ground floors, modular units, perforated walls, *brise-soleil* screens and eaves, transparency of the stairways and ramps. Thus this particular assembly of structures, forms, and functions form the basis of a language that expresses fully the spaces of transition, union, and exchange that weave the rich network of relationships in the university. According to the Venezuelan writer Salvador Garmendía, the University Campus is where "Caracas ... found a unique form of expression in the organization of space ... a sign of identity, and, perhaps, its only lasting creative manifestation."

By rescuing traditional values and applying them in new solutions in the sphere of contemporary design, Villanueva created a model of a city, both local and universal in its scope, where the best features of the utopia of modern urban planning at last became reality.

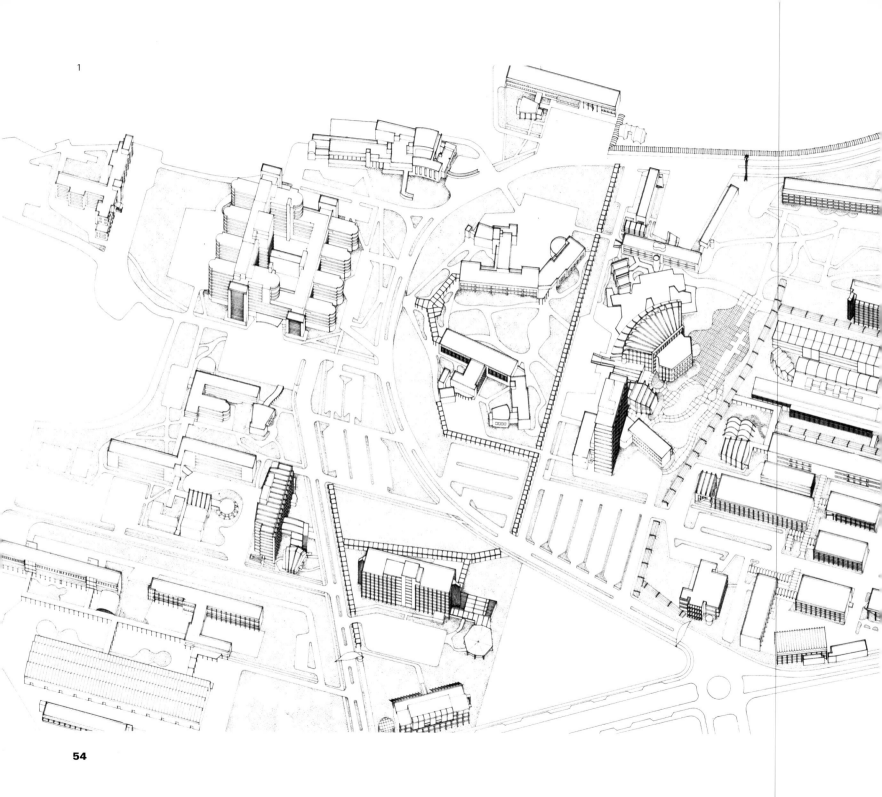

1

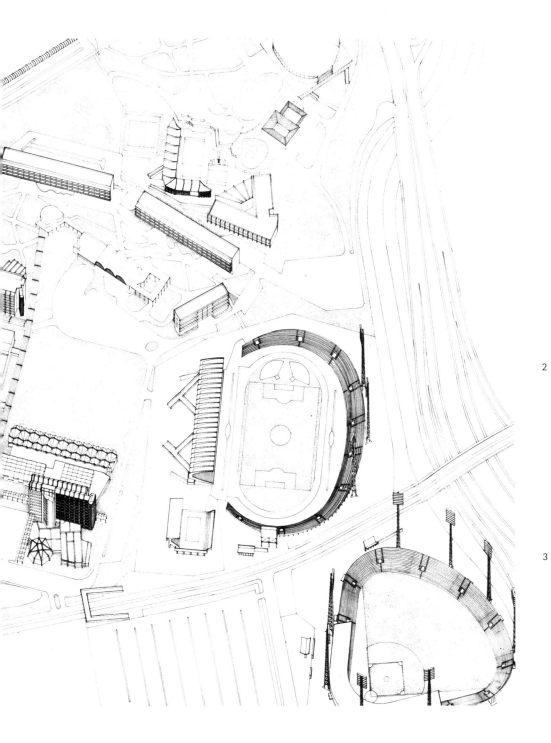

1 Isometric drawing of the University Campus
2 Circulation scheme for pedestrian and automotive traffic
3 Building scheme featuring solids and voids

2

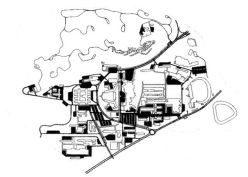

3

University Hospital

University Campus of Caracas
Caracas, Federal District
1945–54
Collaborators: Thomas R. Ponton
Edgar Martin
Developer: Instituto de la Ciudad Universitaria

1 Scheme of the medical area
2 View of the patient wings

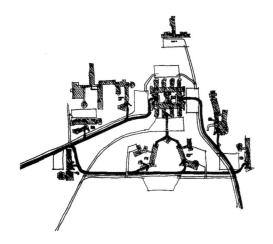

The medical center formed by the Nursing School, the Institutes of Experimental, Anatomical and Pathological Medicine, and the University Hospital served as the foundation of the University Campus of Caracas. All date from 1945 to 1946 and were built in the area that would later be completed with the Institutes of Tropical Medicine and Hygiene, the second stage of the Nursing School, and the Schools of Dentistry and Pharmacy (finished at the end of the 1950s).

Because of its size and central location, the University Hospital became the focal point of the main axis of the first site plan, in the line of perspective of the court, now planted with trees, which was formed by the two converging medical institutes. It stood at the head of the campus; to the west, the mountains and the two arms of the medical institutes acted as a backdrop. From there the ellipse of the initial plan unfolded to gather the sports area at the opposite end of the campus, where the airy curves of the Olympic and baseball stadiums link with the sinuous tentacles of the motorway to the east.

The bulk of the hospital building—a double symmetry consisting of two pairs of elevations with similar features but different heights—dissolves into successive pavilion wings and intermediate courts, alternating solid masses and voids that perforate the large volume, the elements designed to bring about the exchange of heat and cool air by unfolding the surface and increasing its perimeter. The result is a very large container with two interior courtyards and a series of lineal bodies or wings running perpendicular to it in an east-west direction, opening a series of galleries to the north and south. The façades of these galleries incorporate four substantial bodies of ramps covered with large radiatorlike concrete lattices. The corridors and galleries linking the wings are also protected with screens to diffuse the dazzling light and ensure natural ventilation, letting the air flow through the perforated blocks to control the high tropical temperatures.

Inside, the volume is broken down into a series of wards for hospitalization, within which the beds are organized in a "fish-bone" pattern that makes it possible for each patient to be isolated within the general unit. The result is a broken line that adds dynamism to the façade and to the continuous gallery that surrounds the perimeter of the building, ending in the curved balconies of the pavilion wings and offering views of the campus and Mount Ávila.

The initial draft design was drawn up with the participation of two North American hospital experts, Dr. Thomas Ponton and engineer Edgar Martin, who were commissioned to design the interior layout of the building to accommodate 1,000 beds.

However, the final design was influenced greatly by Villanueva's and Blasser's previous experience in the design and construction of a series of hospitals in the interior of the country between 1938 and 1942. These were based on two little-known prototype designs—Type A and Type B—which were developed by the Ministry of Public Works and included pavilions with wide galleries ending in curved loggias, sun-protection overhangs, eaves and lattices, and, more importantly, articulated systems that allowed the buildings to grow and evolve over time.

1

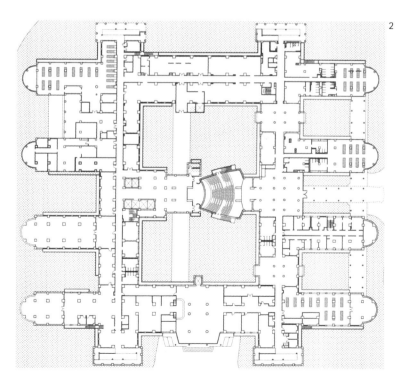

2

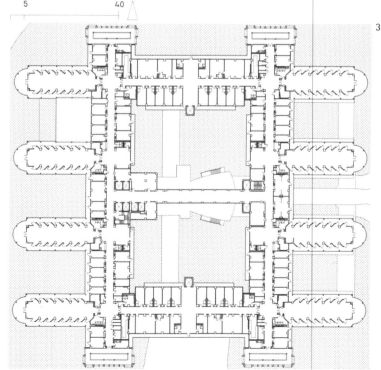

3

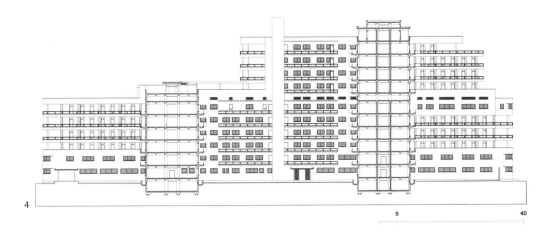

1 View of the east façade
2 Ground floor plan
3 Upper floor plan of hospital wards
4 Cross-section through one of the patios
5 View of the patient galleries and ramps

Olympic Stadium

University Campus of Caracas
Caracas, Federal District
1949–50
Developer: Instituto de la Ciudad Universitaria

1 Olympic and Baseball Stadia complex
2 Detail of the concrete structure, north side

The airy lightness of the Olympic Stadium along with the modest anonymity of the Baseball Stadium adjoining it act as counterweights to the heavy presence of the University Hospital located at the other end of the campus, with their social function serving to create a common area on the limits of the site shared by the university and the city alike.

The elegant simplicity and powerful scale of the Olympic Stadium are articulated in two separate volumes: the shell of the covered grandstand and the half-oval structure of the bleachers. These forceful elements sit opposite each other in a tense yet balanced composition. The whole structure is raised above the ground, where it rests on almost invisible columns that are barely perceptible against the deep shadow of the underside. From this perspective, the body of the central grandstand seems to float above slim columns like the braces of a sail straining in the wind—an effect resulting from the lack of proportion between the twenty-four large V-shaped space frames, placed every 5 meters and joined by a thin 115-meter-long slab, and the small ground supports, which are hidden by the large balcony platform that is also suspended above the ground and connected to the access area by means of light concrete ramps.

According to Sibyl Moholy-Nagy, "in the general context of Villanueva's development, the stadiums signify the transition from the experimental use of reinforced concrete to full mastery over it." This is exemplified by the structural lightness of the bleachers and the unsurpassed elegance of the cantilevered roof over the grandstand, in which the stress moments of the structure and the plasticity of the concrete are fully exploited to create a beautiful form. Crowned by the rhythmic sequence of the concrete cantilevered beams and underlined by the running slab of the balcony that acts as the main access platform, the cylindrical shell of the covered grandstand rises in all its majesty against the silhouette of Mount Ávila to the north and the profile of the city's high-rises to the east.

As in the interior of the Aula Magna Hall, in the stadium the two faces of the folded roof and the bleacher structure fulfill the same objective—that of shaping space on a large scale with a single gesture, without superfluous expressive concessions.

Like the Olympic Stadium, the Baseball Stadium has a seating capacity of 30,000 spectators. However, the continuous ring of concrete that encloses the baseball diamond and the cantilever over the grandstand, which is polished on the outside and has the structure exposed on the underside, differentiate it from the Olympic Stadium and give it a distinct personality.

Despite the fact that they are truly functional works designed for heavy-duty use, each stadium has an indisputable character and appeal that stem from the clear geometry of the design and the frank use of structures and materials. In the pronounced and repeated body of the Olympic Stadium and, later, in the Swimming Pool Complex, the marked contrasts of light and shadow clothe the entire building, forming part of the space. Form is rooted in construction. However, true and beautiful form must be endowed with great expressive freedom, like the single shell of the grandstand in the Olympic Stadium—the constructional clarity of an architectural idea.

1 Panoramic view of the cantilevered roof over the
grandstand looking east towards the city
2 Detail of the access ramps

2

1 Cross section through the structure of the roof and
  the grandstand
2 View from the east
3 Side view of the grandstand

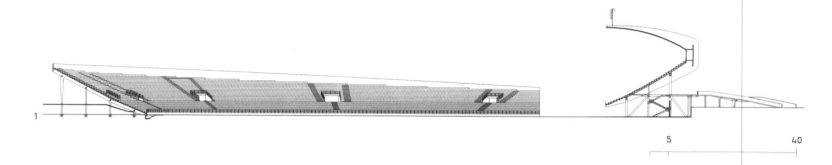

1

5   40

2

Swimming Pool Complex

University Campus of Caracas
Caracas, Federal District
1958–59
Developer: Instituto de la Ciudad Universitaria

1 Detail of the meeting between the two seating tiers
2 Detail of the seating tiers and the roof

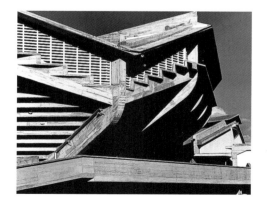

The Swimming Pool Complex was designed on a smaller scale than the other campus sports facilities. However, it was endowed with a monumental strength expressed particularly in the hours of strong sunlight, when it achieves a dramatic effect unequaled by other university buildings—an image captured by Paolo Gasparini's high-contrast photographs.

The main body of the building houses an Olympic swimming pool, a competition diving pool, two wings of tiers forming an L-shaped grandstand and a cafeteria situated on the triangular balcony space above the pools, which serves to articulate the other two bodies of the edifice: the long block with *brise-soleil* screens housing a series of rooms and arenas for different sports, and the high box with a glazed façade accommodating the Olympic gymnastics facilities. The geometric articulation of these volumes around a central space creates a pleasant enclosure against the sculpted hillside. Above, the house of the hacienda estate on which the campus was built is still standing, together with remnants of the chimney of its sugar mill, a free-standing vertical structure visible from the swimming pool area that acts as a counterpoint to the airy towers of the competition diving boards. Like the Olympic Stadium, the whole block of the Swimming Pool Complex is raised one level above the ground to accommodate a service area underneath. Access to the pools is via a pair of concrete ramps that lead up to the balcony platform connected to the lower part of the grandstand, where a wide strip of blazing red glazed panels stands out against the dun gray of the concrete structure, obscured by lines of shadow. Although the floor plan is attractive, the most unexpected and notable feature of the design is its daring articulation of volumes and unusual interplay of exterior and interior spaces. The prowlike angle that resolves the difficult meeting of the two tiers of seating is particularly interesting, as is the fine concrete roof over the grandstand, with its sinuous and suggestive curves. Seen in section or from a foreshortened perspective, the column-beam that supports both the galleries and the roof is reminiscent of a robust, twisted tree opening its branches to the sky.

According to Sibyl Moholy-Nagy, Villanueva faced up to the "timeless challenge of creating art out of structure." Much has been written about the integration of art and architecture, but not about the synthesis of technology and architecture, which was so important in Villanueva's work. Hence the value of structure as the expression of a given material, such as reinforced concrete, and of a way of building that becomes the basis of the design operation. In the Swimming Pool Complex, both the expressive force and the material execution of the structure are the adjectives of a language of figures, textures, and contrasts brought together in a syntax of assembled and modeled elements: on the one hand, the ends of the repeated grandstands—projecting beyond the support beams and the line of angled concrete lattices—that form a system of straight lines; on the other, the curved arrises of the beam-columns and roofs, which throw a shifting shadow that is trimmed and broken up over the exterior surface of the grandstand, folded in space. Built ten years after the Olympic Stadium, the Swimming Pool Complex shows Villanueva's mastery of concrete—the raw material used to shape a living entity whose changing skin breathes with the different hours of the day.

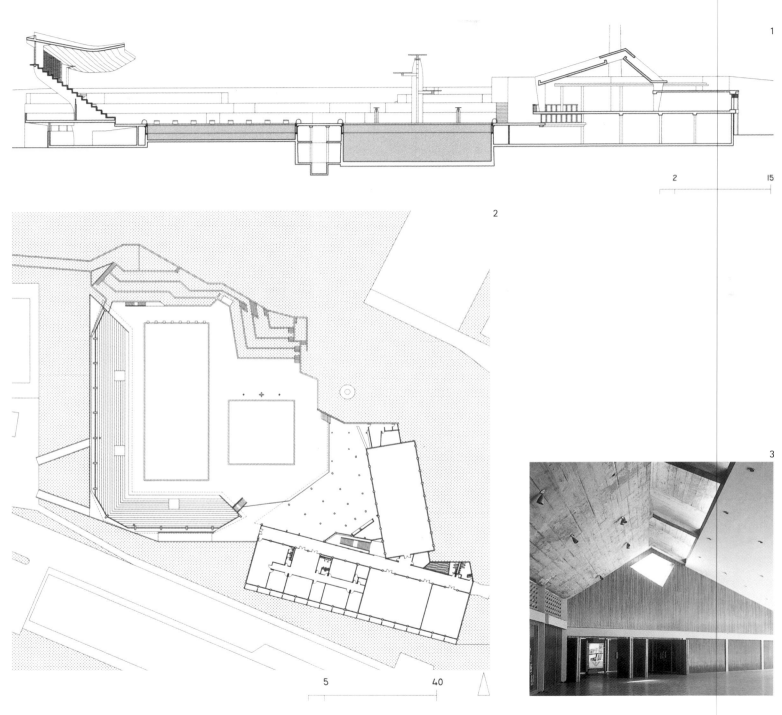

1

2

3

1 Cross section through the pools
2 General floor plan
3 Partial view of the facilities building
4 View from the northeast
5 General view from the north

4

5

2

1 Detail of the seating tiers and the roof
2 Detail of the column-beam supporting the
  cantilevered roof
3 Detail of the concrete roof

3

71

Central Area

University Campus of Caracas
Caracas, Federal District
1952–53
Developer: Instituto de la Ciudad Universitaria

1 Sketch of the complex
2 Aerial view of the complex from the north

The Central Area, designed for administrative and cultural use, is not only the key feature of the University Campus of Caracas but also one of the most important works of contemporary architecture in Venezuela. Formed by several buildings and two plazas, it features the bulk of the works that comprise the "Synthesis of the Arts" project, an endeavor in which a distinguished group of local and foreign artists participated.

Designed and built in just under two years—between 1952 and 1953—the area marked a radical change in the conception of the campus and maturely asserted a new architectural language, expressed through the use of exposed concrete frames and large surfaces of glazed color tiles.

Articulated as a succession of open spaces and buildings running in a north-south direction, the area broke away from the symmetrical arrangement and the east-west orientation imposed by the monumental axis of the first plan for the campus, derived from Beaux Arts traditions, of which the University Hospital was the visible head.

The first elliptical arc formed by the road leading to the University Hospital was maintained, but the second arc, which was intended to be opposite the medical institutes, was replaced by a straight road running in a north-south direction. This new road was conceived as a large covered walkway marking a contrasting horizontal plane of shade to the vertical series of flagpoles that accompany and reinforce the design; this, together with the vehicle entrances to the campus and a small parking lot, definitively separates the two stages of the project. Inside the Central Area, this pedestrian walkway—laid out like a taut, fine, and intangible bowstring, almost as if it were the "legal limit", record or trace of a decision—turns into an interior street that connects different spaces in an uninterrupted succession of plazas, courts, gardens, and buildings, forming a universe that can be explored and discovered in a vitalizing architectural experience.

This continuous and homogenous system of built and unbuilt spaces is succeeded by a wide, open space planted with tropical vegetation and presided over by Balthazar Lobo's *Maternity* sculpture— a landscaped space limited on the other end by a wide covered walkway that overlooks the entire area and marks the place where the Schools of Humanities and Engineering begin.

The spaces encompassed by the Central Area lead on from each other: the Plaza del Rectorado, a square lined on three sides by the Administration Building, housing the Rector's offices, and its two outstretched arms; the Communications Building and the Museum that is flanked by the Clock Tower; the Hall of Honor and the Covered Plaza, an area that opens in several directions and forms a large hall or vestibule to Aula Magna Hall, the core of the complex; the Concert Hall and the red tower of the University Library, which acts as a landmark of the campus; and finally, the parking lot that serves the whole complex.

In this sense, the Central Area is a "space made up of spaces" consisting of interior and exterior areas, a "building made up of buildings" which, despite not having a unitary façade, has a strong and powerful shape.

1

2

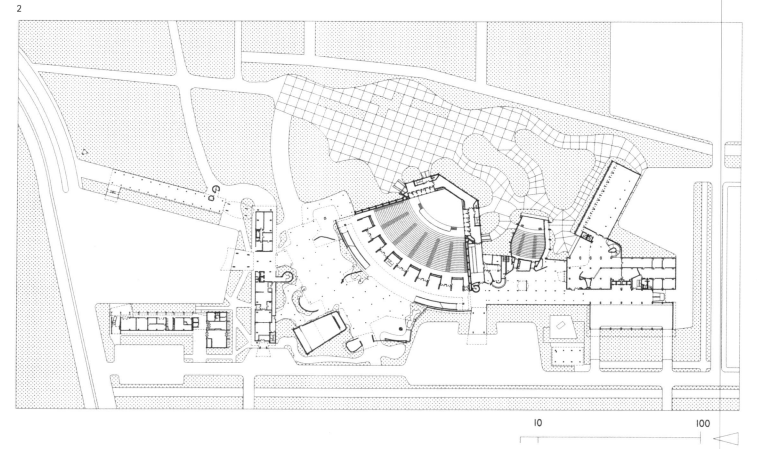

10   100

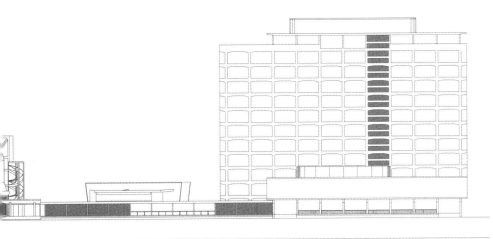

3

1 West elevation of the Central Area
2 Ground floor plan of the Central Area
3 Side view of the complex from the north
4 Circulation flow plan

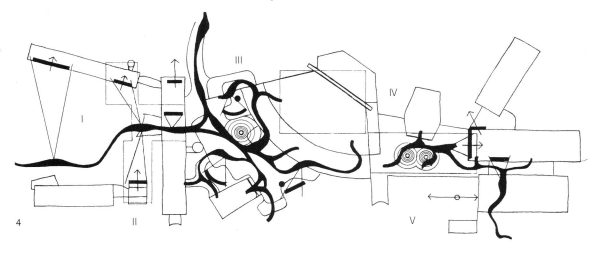

4

| I to V | Movements |
| Static elements |
| Moving elements (movement in the direction of the arrow) |
| Four-dimensional elements |
| Internal spaces |
| Visitor trajectory |

75

Plaza del Rectorado

University Campus of Caracas
Caracas, Federal District
1952–53
Developer: Instituto de la Ciudad Universitaria

1 Internal view of the Clock Tower
2 View of the west façade of the
  Museum Building and the Clock
  Tower

The Plaza del Rectorado is the first area of contact between the city and the university campus. This plaza—together with the buildings that surround it on three sides—acts as the public face of the university, the "courtyard of honor" or government square that asserts the university's autonomy. Originally designed as an access area for pedestrians and cars, it acted as a transport terminal and a parking lot. It was the intersection of pedestrian flow from the student residences and the faculties to the campus bus stop, which stood at the end of the open ground floor of the museum building by the clock tower; there, a canopy (since demolished) together with the Communications Building and the Administration Building, which serves as a large gateway to the Covered Plaza, formed the links between two different systems of circulation, both essential to the design and flow of the campus. Today it is a pedestrian square at one end of which stands a bronze sculpture designed by Francisco Narváez—originally located in the terrace of the Central Library.

On entering via the Plaza Venezuela and the curved arc formed by the side of the hill where the Botanical Gardens are located, the first thing one sees is the clock tower to the left. The tower acts as a landmark to the area, which is bordered on three sides by buildings laid out in a U-shape, open to the north and enclosed by a green wall to which the vault of the covered walkway acts as a plinth. The parallelepiped volume of the Administration building is developed horizontally, on three levels, with regular fenestration piercing the façade. It is lifted from the ground on a tapered base that features two murals by Oswaldo Vigas and is separated from the cylindrical volume of the stairwell at the back. Closed off to the west, it opens up at the eastern end with a balcony that overlooks the gardens surrounding the student residence halls.

The Communications and Student Services Building—perpendicular to the Administration Building—is made up of two bodies: one has walls decorated with a mural designed by Vigas, the other has a grid of perforated concrete panels on its western façade where a series of windows alternate and contrast with deep shadows. The east wing of the museum building forms a narrow, closed line with murals by Vigas and Armando Barrios facing onto the plaza. Connected to the Administration building at an angle by a concrete arch, it is raised one level above an open floor space and is flanked by the symbol of the university: the attractive clock tower formed by three columns rotated in space. The Administration Building acts as the façade of the Central Area, the gateway to the core of the university, and is marked by a large entrance canopy that creates a passage of shade in marked contrast to the dazzling tropical light outside.

The area enclosed by these buildings is a large courtyard open to the sky, a "sunlit plaza" that by way of the large central canopy connects on the other side of the Administration Building with the "shaded plaza" commonly known as the Covered Plaza—a space defined by a wide rounded roof that entraps an area of open and changing perspectives. Whereas the first could be a work of the Renaissance, the second is definitely an invention—a courtyard-cum-garden-cum-street-cum-vestibule; it is the sum of different sensations, the passageway to a new space.

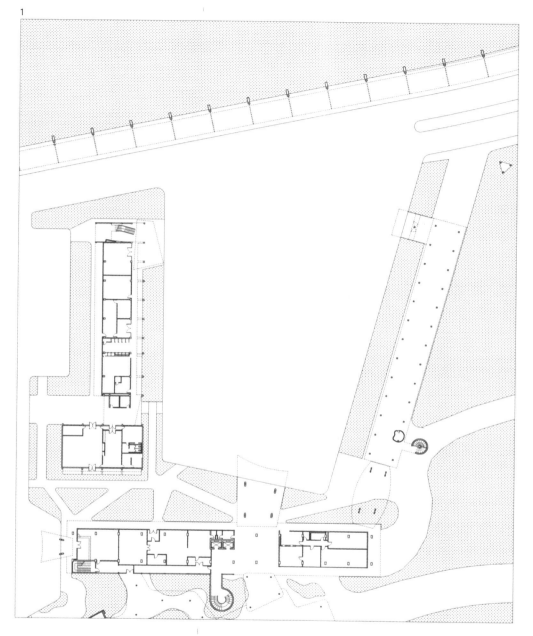

1

2

1 Ground floor of the complex
2 East façade of the Administration Building (Rector's
   Offices)
3 Covered Walkway closing the Plaza, with a sculpture
   by Narváez in the foreground
4 Covered Walkway
5 South façade of the Administration Building, with
   one of the accesses to the Covered Plaza

2   30

3

4

5

Covered Plaza and Covered Walkways

University Campus of Caracas
Caracas, Federal District
1952–53
Developer: Instituto de la Ciudad Universitaria

The Covered Plaza is a discovery, a space stretched in time, a bridge connecting memory and design through past experiences reinterpreted from a new and unifying perspective. It is an invention that participates actively in the construction of a space that is shaped by the experience of moving through it, that changes and rematerializes with each footstep.

As an area of transit and meetings, it is the place where natural and man-made elements converge—an environment uniquely suited for the integration of art and architecture. As an interior plaza, a peaceful and shaded area, it is also the place where several buildings are connected: the Administration Building, the Hall of Honor, Aula Magna Hall, the Concert Hall, and the Central Library. The area unfolds under a large roof of varying heights that derives from the separation of the concrete slabs and opens to the sky to create small islands of light and color for the plants and works of art that are dotted along the undulating perimeter. These intermitent openings contrast with the regular geometry imposed by the lines of the floor, the beams of the canopy structure, and the vertical planes of the columns. The whole is characterized by two large horizontal and parallel planes: the rough, shaded frame of the concrete roof; and the smooth, shining surface of the floor, where the figures inhabiting the space are reflected and multiplied before becoming blurred on the edges of the platforms.

Sculptures such as *Amphion* by Henri Laurens, *Cloud Shepherd* by Jean Arp, and *Dynamism at 30 Degrees* by Anton Pevsner; aluminum and ceramic compositions such as *Positive-Negative and Sophia* by Victor Vasarély; and murals by Fernand Léger, Mateo Manaure, and Pascual Navarro turn the Covered Plaza into a true work of art—an expression of the "conscious correlations" that exist between the objects and subjects that revolve around the time-space dimension of the perimeter marked by the powerful synthesis wrought by Villanueva.

Conceived as a system of musical movements that articulate the journey of the "foot that walks" and the "eye that sees" within a concert of sensations, the function of the static or dynamic elements—of the so-called "four-dimensional" effects of movement as an experience of perspective—is to highlight or camouflage surfaces, disarticulate volumes, accentuate directions, expand space, deepen perspective, and "make the invisible visible." According to Jean Arp, "definitions are variable and intangible, like clouds"—which is why interpreting the musical order that structures this area requires an exercise of abstraction, a language common to architecture and music that is capable of turning music into weightless architecture, as represented by the myth of Laurens's *Amphion*.

This open-air museum is scored by the movement of the body and the survey of the eye. It is surrounded by an atmosphere of vitality, where the delight of perceiving space gives way to a revelation: a work reshaping itself, again and again, as it is viewed from different perspectives.

For Villanueva, the essential qualities of an architect were "an ability to perceive in advance, a capacity to catalyze, an ability to create,"—characteristics exemplified perfectly in this integral work endowed with a clear identity.

Covered Plaza, with Pascual Navarro's mural and the south façade of the Administration Building in the background

1 Plan of the complex
2 Hall of Honor, cross section
3 Aerial view of the Aula Magna Hall, the Covered
  Plaza and the Hall of Honor
4 Hall of Honor, longitudinal section
5 Jean Arp's *Cloud Shepherd* and Mateo Manaure's
  mural

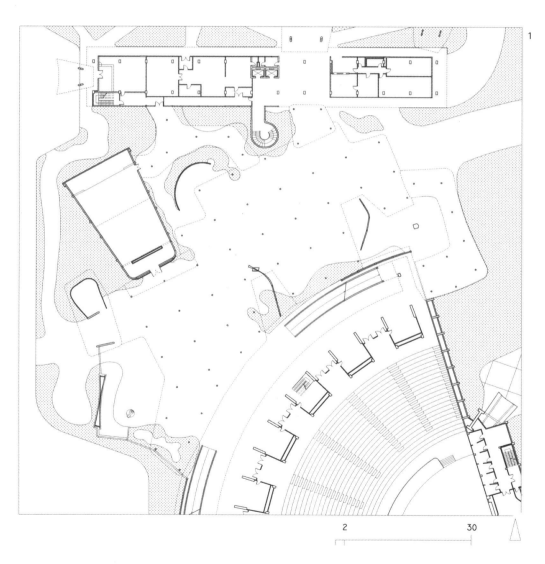

1

2   30

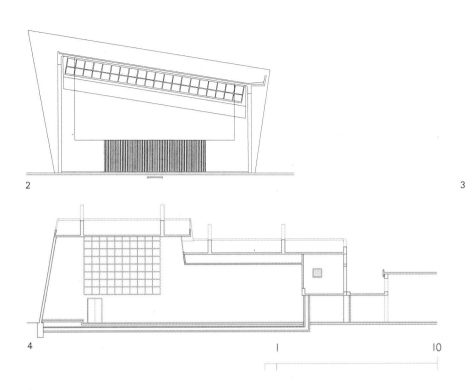

2

4

| 1 | 10 |

3

5

1

2

3

4

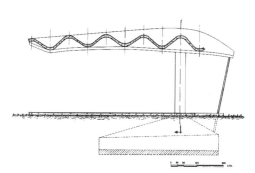

La Arquitectura es Acto Social por excelencia,
Arte utilitario, como proyección de la Vida misma,
ligada a problemas económicos y Sociales y no
únicamente a normas estéticas.
Para ella, la forma no es lo mas importante:
Su principal misión: Resolver hechos humanos.

Su medio expresivo y condicional: el espacio interior,
el espacio útil fluido, usado y gozado por los
hombres: "es una matriz que envuelve Vida".
Es Arte del Espacio a dentro y afuera, Arte
Abstracto y no Representativo, pero con una
función y esencia de lógica Cartesiana.
                    Carlos Raul Villanueva
Caracas, 22/12/67*

Architecture is a social act *par excellence*; a utilitarian art, a projection of life itself, linked to social and economic problems and not only to aesthetic norms.
In architecture, form is not what matters most. Its principal mission is to solve human needs.
Its expressive and conditional medium is interior space, the serviceable, fluid space that is used and enjoyed by man. "It is the womb that envelops life." It is the art of interior and exterior space, an abstract rather than representational art, but with a function and essence of Cartesian logic.

Carlos Raúl Villanueva
Caracas, 22/12/67

Covered Walkways

If the covered plaza can be said to have its source in the garden-court, the covered walkway has its origin in the corridors of houses and city arcades. Nevertheless, they owe their appearance to the attention and role that modern urban planning gives to pedestrian and car traffic.

An essential part of daily life on the campus, covered walkways are the physical manifestation of paths left by innumerable feet circulating in a free flow in directions that have defined an autonomous layout independent of that of the buildings. They house multiple activities beneath their canopies and express—with their own attributes and characteristics—the most emblematic image of the university.

As the manifestation of circulation raised to the level of architecture, they display a wide and surprising range of shapes and structural solutions, designed by the engineers Otaola and Benedetti, as well as an admirable sequence of spatial, and in some cases, acoustic effects. With spans of up to 15 meters between supports, daring cantilevered vaults of almost 9 meters, and a total length of more than 1.5 kilometers, these expressive walkways play a fundamental role in the campus as an unprecedented model of urban development that functions with a vitality and personality of its own.

On the left, structural section and cantilevered concrete structure of the Covered Walkways

Aula Magna Hall

University Campus of Caracas
Caracas, Federal District
1952–53
Developer: Instituto de la Ciudad Universitaria

1 Sketch
2 Access ramps

Aula Magna Hall is a true architectural, sculptural, and human space. Modern and stark, it is stripped to the bare essentials. As Sibyl Moholy-Nagy wrote, it is "a festive and lyrical celebration of space … an intended appeal to individual mood." The interior both dazzles the senses and inspires awareness. Bruno Zevi and Villanueva both believed that "the specific expression of architecture is built space." In the Aula Magna, space has been measured and proportioned in a clean, direct way that lacks neither grandeur nor monumentality and creates a dense and full atmosphere.

According to Villanueva: "From the essential invention of space as the key of the entire project, the volumetric enclosure articulates itself. It defines and harmonizes the third architectural element: structure." The Aula Magna is a space to be discovered, strongly protected by the structure that acts as its skeleton, sustains it without intrusion, and guards an interior of immense and finely tuned resonances. Villanueva's space is augmented by the work of Alexander Calder, whose colorful floating clouds, "flying saucers" as he referred to them, fill the auditorium, radiating waves of sound in this culminating work of the "Synthesis of the Arts" project.

The Aula Magna is the largest and the most important of the university's fifteen auditoriums. The wide, fan-shaped floor plan has seating capacity for more than 2,500 people between the orchestra stalls and the interior balcony that sweeps over them—without actually touching the side walls—in an airy and defiant curve. The acoustic shapes designed by Calder and adapted by the engineer Robert Newman hang from the ceiling and lean against the side walls; suspended in space, they seem to rise and fall with the varying intensity of the double fluorescent and incandescent lamp reflectors in the ceiling. These eyes of light create an atmosphere of blue and cast a warm light over the orchestra stalls, and together with the sculpture, augment and expand the space into a universe that is already present in Calder's first *Constellations*.

Aula Magna Hall is connected to the Covered Plaza by a system of double doors between the hall and the vestibule area, and by a large circular corridor with two pairs of ramps leading up to the exterior balcony. This large, curved arc together with the cantilevered roof that covers this area is connected to that of the plaza, leaving a line of light over the modeled concrete surface of the roof. The light and shadows that project over both the surfaces and the people create a space of movement and an atmospheric sculpture made of emptiness and transparencies.

The roof was designed in the shape of a seashell by the Danish engineering firm Christiane & Nielsen. It has twelve inverted-L columns with 45-meter spans that lean on a large structural frame with the "drawing" of the exposed structure showing on the beams and the side walls. The rough connection of several blind bodies on the outside stands in contrast to the fluid and lucid unity of the interior, a latent space guarding a large stabile in perpetual movement.

The Aula Magna is a masterpiece. When referring to the architectural framework that gave birth to the "Synthesis of the Arts" experience, Villanueva used to say that "the final result always reflects the unique meaning of an exceptional piece …, an unrepeatable combination of propitious conditions."

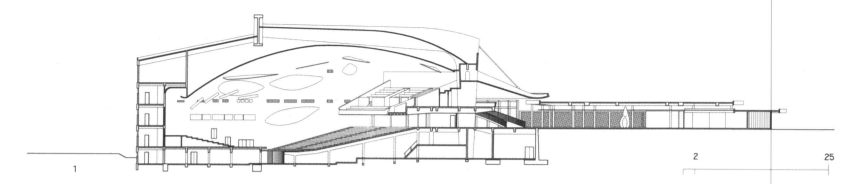

1

2   25

1 Longitudinal section
2 Ground floor plan
3 Upper floor plan
4 View of the east façade, with access to the
  Covered Plaza
5 Roof structure

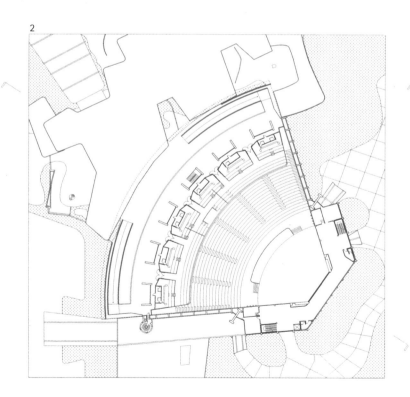

2

3

5   40

4

5

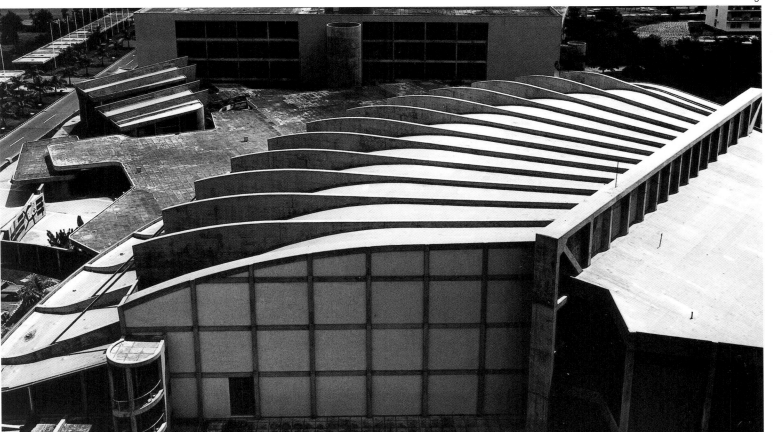

1 Access ramps seen from the upper balcony
2 Concourse, meeting of the Covered Plaza and the
  Aula Magna access ramps
3 Foyer with perforated block screens to ensure
  natural lighting

2

3

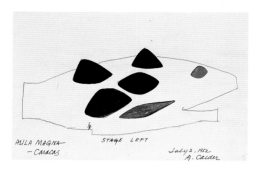

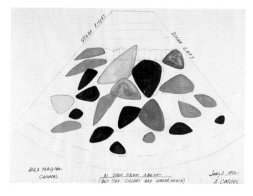

Above, sketches of Alexander Calder's acoustic *Flying Saucers*

Right, interior of Aula Magna Hall

1

2

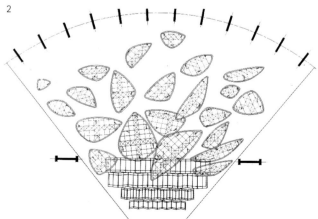

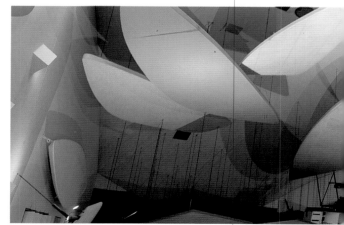

1 Interior with balcony
2 Constructive scheme of the *Flying Saucers*
3 Contained movement of the *Flying Saucers*
4 Detail of the entrance doors to Aula Magna Hall
5 Detail of the fastening of the *Flying Saucers*

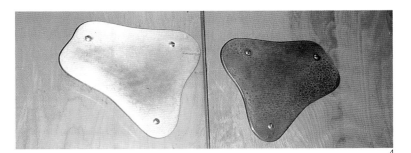

4

5

3

Concert Hall

University Campus of Caracas
Caracas, Federal District
1952–53
Developer: Instituto de la Ciudad Universitaria

Located between the massive bodies of Aula Magna Hall and the Central Library, the modest structure of the Concert Hall is barely perceptible through the concrete screens of the walkway that leads to it. In the open it looks like a mass anchored in the dock of the plaza and put to rest on the grass behind this group of buildings, presided over by Balthazar Lobo's sculpture *Maternity*, where it stands out as much for its continuous shape as for the attractive mural designed by Mateo Manaure, which sets it off against the green. Designed for soloists and small groups of performers, it was built on a more intimate scale than the Aula Magna but equipped with a similar acoustic quality, which highlights individual instruments and voices.

To respond to the acoustic requirements, the hall was fitted with a double roof. As in many of Villanueva's buildings, the outer roof is formed by a continuous concrete slab suspended from large structural frames. This structure acts as a necessary support to the protected and modulated space inside. In contrast, the free-floating acoustic ceiling inside is made of wood slats arranged in a band that slopes from the back of the hall to the back of the stage and ends short of the bare side walls, where two lines of indirect lighting delineate the small wall sculptures designed by Manaure. The ceiling directs the eye to the modest stage and resembles a waterfall—a musical wave made visible that flows from the performers out over the orchestra stalls.

In the Concert Hall the use of wood is reminiscent of its warm treatment in the work of Alvar Aalto. In the Aula Magna it serves to mark the stage, delineating an area next to a suspended frame articulated in light and dark panels—a reflecting plane for projecting sound.

The Concert Hall is a refined coordination of space and form thematically similar to the auditoriums that serve the different faculties and schools of the university. It employs an architectural system in which different programatic spaces are linked sequentially, in which interior function is expressed on the exterior, and which creates optimal conditions for the "Synthesis of the Arts" project.

At the entrance to the hall, the area of the walkway leading from the Covered Plaza spreads out to form a wide vestibule defined on the entrance façade near the doors to the hall by a long mural designed by Pascual Navarro. At the end, against the Central Library wall above a mural designed by Manaure there is a window of light in the roof to separate it from the tower. In the center of the area, in a hexagonal patio near Victor Vasarély's sculpture *Positive-Negative*, a folded, perforated plane of aluminum plays with the contrast of lights and shadows that, together with those produced by the perforated concrete wall and the transparency of the architecture, direct the eye to an expression of pure architectural kinetics. At the front of the area, a balcony with a concrete railing opens onto a small exterior garden-court that revolves around Anton Pevsner's sculpture *Dynamism at 30 Degrees* as well as the cubic block of the cooling tower, which is raised on columns and flanked by the vertical planes of the surrounding palm trees, with Vasarély's mural *Sophia*. It is this synthesis with nature, as in Roberto Burle-Marx's splendid landscaping works, that Villanueva describes as an "authentic plastic work, carried out with a new material, a living material."

Interior of the Concert Hall from the entrance

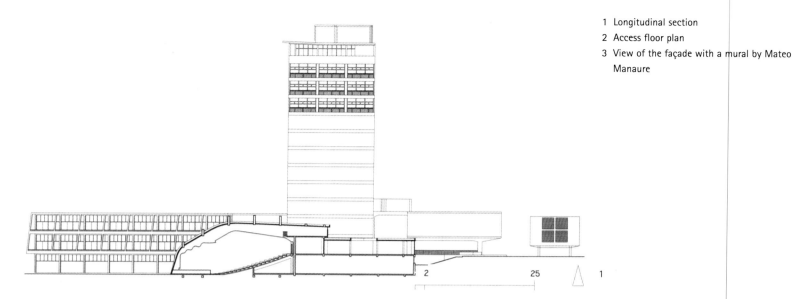

1 Longitudinal section
2 Access floor plan
3 View of the façade with a mural by Mateo
Manaure

2   25   △   1

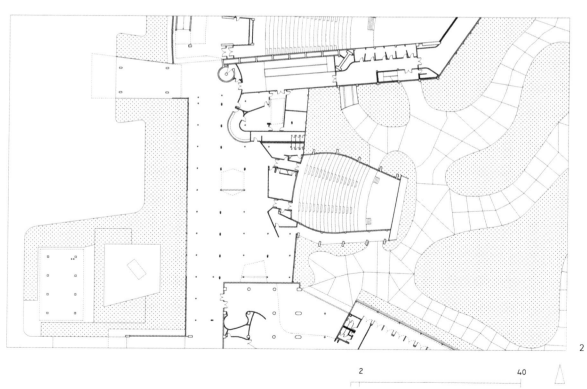

2   40   △   2

3

1 *Positive-Negative* by Victor Vasarély
2 View of the Cooling Tower from the foyer
3 Public space that acts as foyer of the Concert Hall

3

Central Library

University Campus of Caracas
Caracas, Federal District
1952–53
Developer: Instituto de la Ciudad Universitaria

1 Lobby with stained-glass window by Fernand Léger
2 View of the north façade

The Central Library building closes the Central Area of the university campus to the north with its solid cubic bulk and its vibrant chromaticism. It is both an icon of the university in its role as a repository of knowledge and a forceful image of the commitment of architecture to act as a faithful expression of contemporary life. The twelve-story tower, a closed box clad in crimson tiles, shares a theme in common with other Villanueva buildings: a "drawing" resulting from the exposed structural frame of concrete beams and columns on its four façades that acts as the constructional fingerprint of an architectural sign in the face of a large sculptural object. In this respect, it is a foretaste of the colored cubes designed for the Montreal Expo, although it does not make the leap in scale or erase the codes that enable it to be understood as a building.

The Central Library is a brave work of architecture in which the abstract and simplified language used to create its unitary image is its main attraction and at the same time its main virtue, articulating an uncompromising structure that complies with a highly specific program. The function of storing and preserving books requires a closed shape—a large container that provides protection against the environment and ensures the safety of the collection, resolving climatic problems of light and humidity as well as functional problems of shelter and accessibility.

The axis of the tower's rectangular floor plan is oriented in the same north-south direction as the Central Area. On the northern and eastern sides the crimson paneling in its top three floors is replaced by recessed windows that create long, gallerylike balconies protected by concrete slabs that serve as overhangs and finish off the slightly sloped projecting roof of the top floor, which was originally given over to a cafeteria opening onto two terraces at either end. In the lower part of the building, on the west side, a windowless wing raised one level above the ground creates a portico that originally acted as the entrance for vehicle traffic and opened an uninterrupted field of vision between the covered walkway and the lift hall.

Breaking the sequence of the axis established by the Covered Plaza and detaching itself from the tower at an angle is the low wing of the reading rooms, which rests loosely on columns above the garden. This body is developed on two levels that jut out like balconies in search of light and the distant views of the mountain. All of these volumes are linked by the key aspect of the design: the area of the library entrance hall that connects the Covered Plaza, the library tower, and the reading rooms. In this double-height space, a beautiful and unusual double staircase articulates the turn and movement of the body of the halls and gives way to a two-story-high tympanum filled with the exuberant vegetation, light, and color of the stained-glass window designed by Fernand Léger, which is mirrored and reflected on the polished floor of the entrance lobby.

Abstraction animates the contemporary architectural forms of the campus and the geometrical shapes of its artworks. Light and color become a powerful force in the hands of Villanueva, who believes that everything can be changed by color and who sees in Léger's stained-glass window "an orchestra of light." According to Léger, color "is a natural necessity, like water and fire."

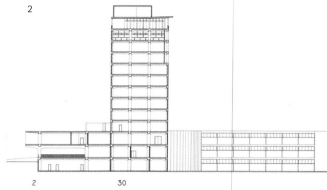

2   30

1 View of the north and west façades
2 Cross section through the tower
3 Ground floor plan
4 Reading room balcony-gallery

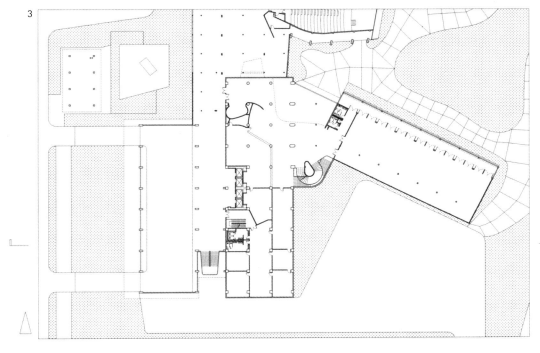

3

2   30

4

School of Humanities

University Campus of Caracas
Caracas, Federal District
1953–56
Developer: Instituto de la Ciudad Universitaria

The School of Humanities accommodates several faculties and institutes that share facilities and administrative offices, making the complex a lively microcosm of the university at large. The horizontal development of the design unfolds in a complex weave of bodies and sections, a series of repeated spaces with patios and inner gardens interspersed between the buildings and offices to create a rich tapestry of areas of circulation and exchange.

Situated at the geographical center of the campus, it is in an area of transition and transit. This is reflected in its interior, a space crossed by corridors, ramps, and staircases that relate the building to an exterior surrounded on all four sides by the covered walkways that direct the pedestrian flows of the campus. The area given over to circulation is as important as the space designed for formal education. The inevitable dialectic between philosophers, lawyers, and writers transcends the lecture rooms and is developed in chance encounters in other areas of the school—in the small squares or agoras, with their cafeterias, and in the corridors lined with bookstores and a wide assortment of facilities that turn them into public streets in the truest sense of the word.

Several elements stand out in this group of one- and two-story buildings: the library of the School of Humanities, with its lightly curved roof; the library of the School of Psychology, which opens out onto a small interior garden with reliefs by Jean Arp and a mural by Sophie Taeuber-Arp; and the striking Auditorium, with its rough concrete walls and large polychromy of red triangles designed by the Venezuelan artist Víctor Valera. Also worthy of note are the ramps and staircases that, because of their combination of designs of concrete blocks and lattices, form dynamic oases of color and movement. The resulting play of light and shadow projected on the walls competes with the abstract characters of Valera's murals, of which there are fifteen throughout the complex.

However, the most dominant and striking element is the long two-story wing of lecture rooms situated to the north. It initially opened onto the gardens of the student residences opposite the evocative patio of *chaguaramos* (architectonic palm trees) at the other end of which the School of Economics was later built.

The layout of this wing has a clear antecedent in Villanueva's design for the Gran Colombia School, built in 1939 around a patio, with the double body of classrooms placed between the area of circulation—from which it was accessed via wide shaded corridors—and the wall opposite the patio, separated from the street by an embankment planted with trees and overlooked by the balconies of the classrooms. In the School of Humanities, it is equally gratifying to see the lecture rooms open onto a garden that offers views of one of the exterior covered walkways, from which the distinct groups of students can in turn be seen in their classrooms.

The School of Humanities is a space that fosters relationships. A dense and branched area designed to facilitate encounters and conversations, it recreates the first moment in which a man seated beneath a tree began to speak and others gathered to listen—the origin of the processes of teaching and learning and the very idea of what a university should be.

Aerial view of the west façade

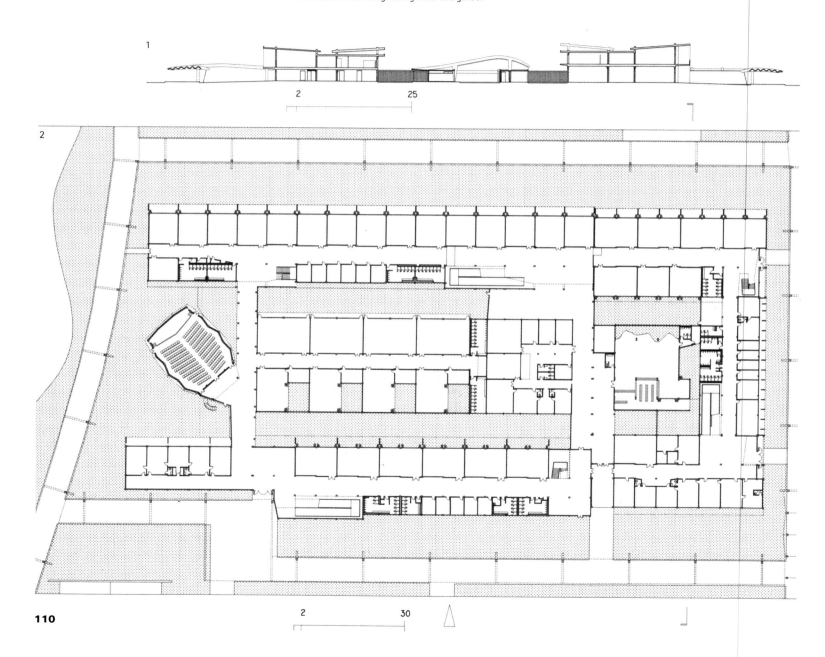

1 Cross section
2 Ground floor plan
3 Inside view of the staircase nucleus
4 Inside view of the ramp nucleus
5 Lecture room wing facing onto the garden

1

2   25

2

110

2   30

3

4 5

School of Architecture

University Campus of Caracas
Caracas, Federal District
1954–57
Developer: Instituto de la Ciudad Universitaria

1 Detail of the *brise-soleils*
2 View of the west façade

In the School of Architecture, Villanueva transcended the limits of the tried and tested. For Sibyl Moholy-Nagy, Villanueva's works are "tentative statements," searches for himself that beyond their architectural manifestation convey a vigilant creative commitment to the mastery of a new language learned through the experiences of everyday life.

After the experience of the Central Area, the School of Architecture presented Villanueva with the most appropriate medium through which to demonstrate his convictions, capacity for experimentation, and ability to redefine the status quo.

Because of his desire to learn as well as to teach, Villanueva presented the building as an architectural exercise and an open lesson for the teachers and students who would live in and share its spaces.

The building consists of a slender nine-story tower around which the lower wings are grouped and arranged in an irregular topography of folded roofs and projecting sections that cover the ample area of the ground floor. This is organized into large units: the entrance and elevator areas, the cafeteria and garden, the auditorium and exhibition hall, and the visual design and composition workshops. The lecture rooms and administration offices are located in the tower.

The tower is a rectangular sculpture of unfolded planes and changing faces. A grid of concrete *brise-soleils* covers the north side, housing the lecture rooms; a fine weave of perforated concrete screens veils the south side, accommodating the extensive circulation area on each floor; a slim staircase of fine vertical concrete strips stands out on the east side; and on the southwest, a crenellated elevator and stair tower rises, alongside blind walls clad with a black, white, and blue tile polychromatic design by the Venezuelan painter Alejandro Otero.

The lower body is an explosion of shapes and spaces that create a changing landscape of prismatic roofs that act as windows of light. Its character results from the structure of repeated folded and triangular slabs that serves as a framework for the transition from exterior to interior, as a measurement of the limits and proportions of the space, and as a support for the ideas turned into architecture. It is the structure that accommodates the small grid—the weave that shapes the form. Together with the works of art, it is the integration of all the elements that form the visual education of an architect.

According to Juan Pedro Posani, Villanueva developed a subtle way of "breaking up geometry" and cutting through articulations—a slow labor of rupture and disarticulation that is evident in the initial sketches of the design. This is a way of reshaping form in a process that passes from the simple, orthogonal, and stable figure, the dominant axis and symmetrical position, the modern "classical" composition to an articulated redistribution, separated into parts, rotated, and displaced, at the same time in flow and in tension.

The School of Architecture is a lesson and a design in progress, an invitation to the participation of thought and use; an homage to architecture itself.

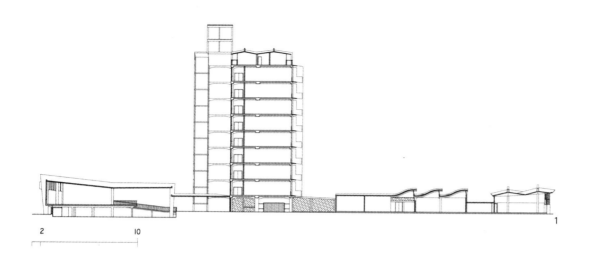

2   10

5   50

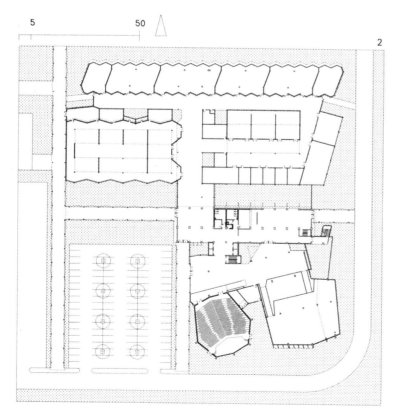

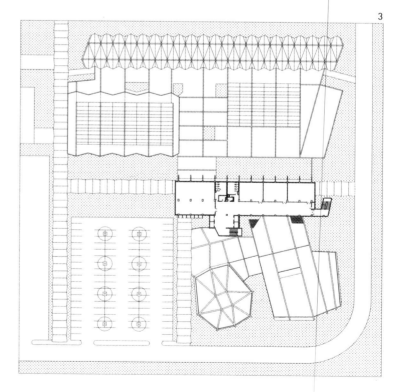

1 Cross section through the exhibition hall
2 Ground floor plan of the complex
3 Typical floor plan of the tower with the roofs of the ground floor
4 Detail of the emergency staircase
5 East façade with emergency staircase
6 Partial view of the workshops, north façade
7 North façade with roof gaps to enable the entry of natural light into the workshops

4

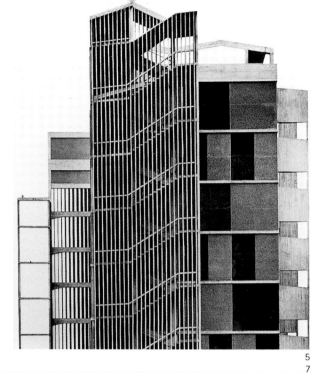

5

6

7

115

1 Pergola and interior garden-patio on the ground
  floor
2 Partial view of the exhibition space, mezzanine level
  with works by Alexander Calder and a mural by
  Víctor Valera
3 Partial view of the workshops
4 Partial view of the exhibition space, lower floor,
  currently part of the library
5 Interior of the architectural design workshop

1

2

3

4

5

I almost feel prouder of my spiritual work, that is, the product of my teaching activity, than of my material *oeuvre*, since nearly all the young architects who have been trained in the country, and whom I regard as my spiritual children, have been my disciples.

Carlos Raúl Villanueva
Caracas, 18/9/64

School of Dentistry

University Campus of Caracas
Caracas, Federal District
1955–58
Developer: Instituto de la Ciudad Universitaria

Typologically, the School of Dentistry belongs to the building typology of the tower, which is common to the university campus. In this respect, it shares certain features with the tower of the School of Architecture; both are far removed from the more modest and less accomplished schemes of the Schools of Pharmacy and Economics.

Unlike most of the university buildings, which stand in a north-south orientation, the School of Dentistry has an east-west siting. On the west elevation, a large concrete overhang crowns the top floor and drops vertically, encasing the broken planes of the façade while forming a large frame for the different colored spandrels and rows of small, high windows of the bathrooms and service areas. This side of the building acts as an environmental insulator, making it possible for this space studded with stairs and areas of circulation to breathe through a skin of perforated concrete screens.

A typical floor plan of the ten-story tower features a series of lecture rooms that open to the east on one side and to an interior corridor on the other. This corridor is connected to the differently sized service areas and the auxiliary staircases that form the shorter, more irregular body of the west façade.

The *brise-soleils* on the east side of the building are formed by a series of horizontal planes of concrete developed along the whole length of the building and connected by slim concrete braces, giving the appearance of a series of repeated eaves. These sun shades stand in contrast to the *brise-soleils* on the north façade of the School of Architecture, which are formed by long, vertical planes of concrete broken by transparent voids at floor level that, when seen from different angles, seem superimposed, accentuating the effect of perspective.

According to Venezuelan architect Juan Pedro Posiani, the "optical multiplicity" that characterises the façades of Villanueva's buildings is always striking. This is particularly true of the façades of the School of Architecture and the School of Dentistry, where the separation and articulation of volumes gives rise to a series of visual effects that derive from the textures of the structures and materials used: the large windowless surfaces of concrete and perforated planes of concrete lattice; the vertical surfaces clad in colorful glazed tiles (a complete work of art that transforms Alejandro Otero's *Color Rhythms* into the key for reading the rhythmic sequences of the architectural elements present in the façades of the School of Architecture or the balanced accents of color produced by Omar Carreño's polychromies in the School of Dentistry); the distinctive pattern of the window frames; the varying designs of the sun-shade solutions represented by the concrete-and-metal *brise-soleils*; and the characteristic "drawing" produced by the exposed structural frame, which weaves and unites all the elements in an all-embracing *Gestalt*.

On the ground level, one of the most attractive spaces of the building is the entry area, formed by an open space between inside and outside. It is partly roofed over and partly covered with a pergola that connects it to the garden. Above this light horizontal plane, the free-standing auditorium rises from the ground revealing the broken line of its free-floating stalls.

View of the north and west façades

1

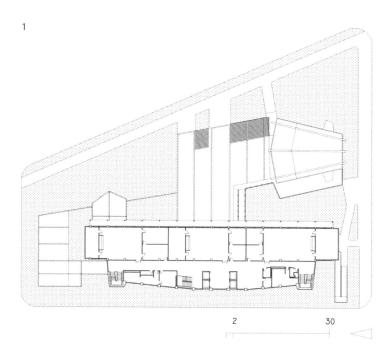

2

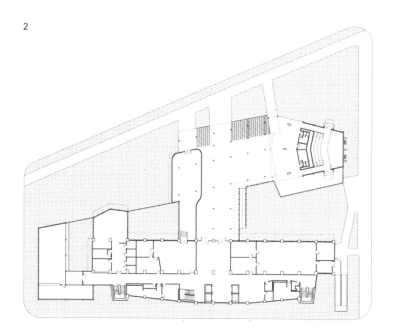

2   30

122

3

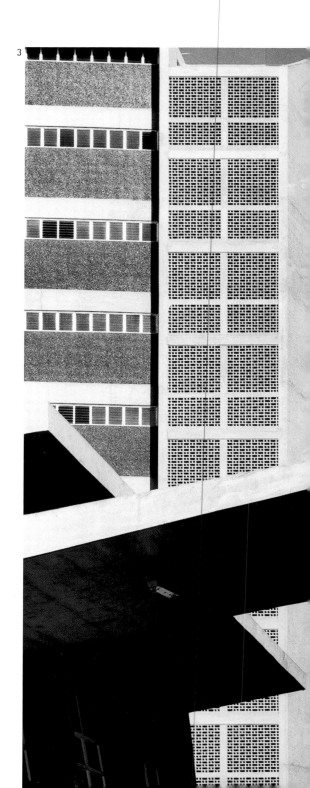

1 Typical floor plan of the tower
2 Ground floor plan of the complex
3 View of the west façade, with the canopy of
   the Nursing School in the foreground
4 Covered access to the tower and the hall of
   the auditorium

4

1 Exterior garden-patio between the tower and the auditorium
2 Partial view of the east façade with the auditorium in the foreground

School of Petroleum Engineering

University of Zulia
Maracaibo, Zulia State
1956–57
Developer: Universidad de Zulia

The School of Petroleum Engineering forms part of the Faculty of Engineering of the University of Zulia, which is located in Maracaibo, in the western part of the country next to Lake Maracaibo, an area renowned for its hot and humid climate.

The horizontal complex consists of seven buildings spread out over a wide, open area. Organized along a north-south axis of pedestrian traffic—a wide covered walkway that acts as the backbone of the campus, connecting the buildings and distributing the circulation flows between them—it is surrounded by roads and parking lots

An auditorium, a cafeteria, a library, and four long buildings with their main façades looking in a north-south direction that house administrative offices, lecture rooms, and laboratories converge in a site whose plan echoes that of the school in the Rafael Urdaneta Development (built ten years earlier), also in Maracaibo. This school has a wide double corridor connecting four wings of classrooms lined with corridors on both sides and interspersed with court-gardens, articulating a layout of repeated isolated units that respond to the demands of the environment and remain open to future growth by stages.

Several features of the School of Petroleum Engineering stand out: the exposed frame of beams above the roof of the auditorium (which relates it to those of the Concert Hall and the Hall of Honor at the University Campus of Caracas); the cafeteria and library, which incorporate gardens; and the units formed by the two-level, 100-meter-long buildings that incorporate buffer spaces and interior walkways with stairs at each end. Elements of climatic adaptation are in evidence everywhere: in the combination of recessed lower floors and projecting upper sections that create shaded areas along the lower walls; the long, continuous lines of moveable, vertical metal lattices painted in vibrant colors on the south sides of some buildings, forming air chambers to fight off the heat; the fine skin of sinuous perforated concrete walls that cover the rest of the buildings and even the stairwells, turning the interiors into bright and gratifying spaces.

The buildings are formed by a skeleton and a skin. Given Villanueva's predilection for reinforced concrete, with its technological and expressive possibilities, the structures and perforated concrete wall panels are presented free of cladding: their dull gray material appears naked with all of its imperfections and modesty, but also with all the strength and charm of its texture, open to the caress of the hand and the gaze of the eye.

As in other works, the characteristic "Villanueva block," repeated in long, continuous surfaces and framed by the structure, dims the harsh tropical light, is conducive to air circulation, and ensures the cross-ventilation that is one of the virtues of traditional architecture—an architecture that was simply attuned to the regional characteristics.

Whether it is the expression of an identity, the successful use of a language of luminous contrasts, or the response to a given climate, for Villanueva this work represented a commitment to built architecture rather than the end result of a creative act.

Façade with mobile metal louvers

1

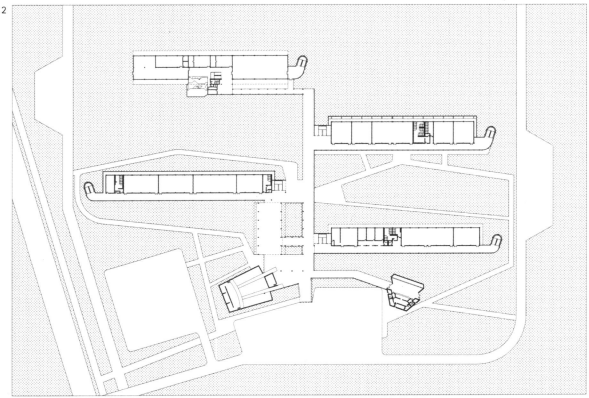

2

1 View from the southeast
2 Floor plan of the complex
3 and 4 Interior and exterior views of the stair
  nucleus

3

4

Museum of Fine Arts

Los Caobos
Caracas, Federal District
1935–36
1952
1966–76
Collaborator (extension): Oscar Carmona
Developer: Ministry of Public Works

In the Museum of Fine Arts several buildings come together in one: the first museum dating from 1935; the first extension executed in 1952; and the second and more important extension, designed in 1966, inaugurated in 1973, and finally opened to the public ten years later, in 1976.

The first museum, together with the Maracay buildings, belongs to Villanueva's early historicist period—a stage during which his designs were directly influenced by his training at the Ecole des Beaux Arts in Paris. These first works were the product of both the cultural tastes of Venezuelan society and his personal situation at the time. They were conscious approximations, lucid approaches to reality, and necessary adjustments to shared values that used an academic language typical of his training and could be easily understood and accepted but at the same time recognized national tradition. For Sibyl Moholy-Nagy, the charm of the original museum lies in the "indoor-outdoor rhythm of its rooms." These were organized following the typological layout of a house with a central patio, exterior access galleries, and interior galleries arranged around a court. Circulation flows were interwoven between these areas and the halls, passing from the bright atmosphere of the patio to the mellow light of the high-ceilinged exhibition halls that were illuminated from above through modulated skylights.

Designed with a simple neoclassical language, the whiteness of the museum highlights the delicate balance of the different elements that form the lovely patio and pleasant proportions of the halls and galleries. When the Science Museum was built next to it at a later date, the two buildings were arranged symmetrically to create a balanced composition around an open circular space, with the front gallery of the Science Museum and the back gallery of the Museum of Fine Arts facing the curve. Although their schemes differed, both buildings unfolded their urban façades to "amplify" through perspective the scale and the symbolic value of these museums whose programs were really rather modest.

The first extension to the original building added a patio, an auditorium, new halls, storerooms, and administrative offices, as well as a small outdoor café that was later demolished. The two colonnaded portals and the curved wall of the rear façade disappeared to create a sense of continuity between the area and the interior galleries and patio, the paving of which was replaced with grass around the central pond. With the new exhibition spaces, the galleries—which were previously integrated into the halls in the exhibition circuit—achieved greater independence, reasserting the "circulation" facet of their character as a result of their new position in relation to the patio. Several years later they would be reinterpreted and reapplied in the final design of the Jesús Soto Museum.

1 Preliminary sketch of the second extension
2 Aerial view of the museum complex

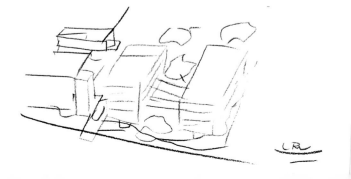

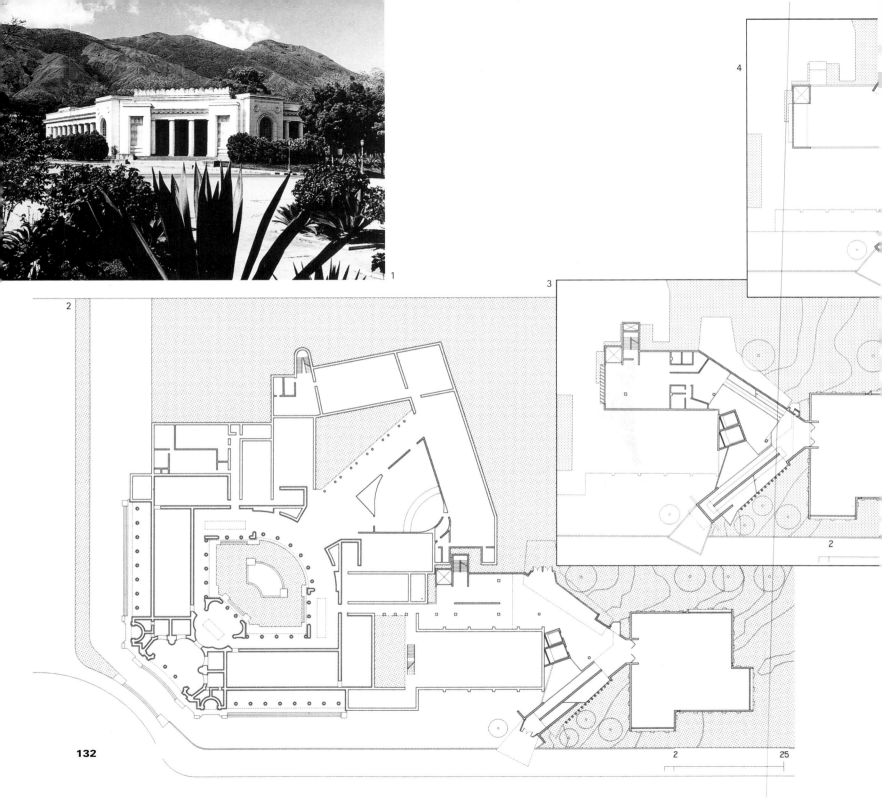

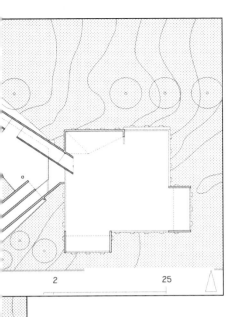

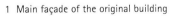

1 Main façade of the original building
2 Ground floor plan of the complex
3 Typical floor plan, second extension
4 Plan of the terrace, second extension
5 Courtyard of the original building
6 View of the ensemble, with the plaza and the
  Museum of Natural Sciences on the right

1, 2 and 3 Picture windows of exhibition rooms 6, 2,
    and 1 looking out over Los Caobos Park
4 Longitudinal section, second extension
5 and 6 Views of the model, photographic montage

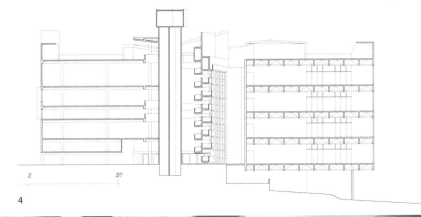

4

5

6

The second extension is a museum in its own right. Built thirty years after the original edifice, it was one of the last works designed by Villanueva, with the collaboration of the architect Oscar Carmona and the engineers W. Zalewzky, J. A. Peña, and T. Brzezinski. The concrete building used a strong language marked by the exposed structure and the distinctive assembly of prefabricated and post-tensed elements. It was developed vertically to avoid cutting down the tall trees of Los Caobos park, with a floor plan that adapted well to the original museum. The tower was organized into three units. The first unit houses the administration and management offices, facilities, and small exhibition halls in one body. The second, a square 21 x 21-meter volume, houses the exhibition halls, one on top of the other. These include the experimental hall on the lower ground floor (which opens out to the exterior sculpture garden and then to the sculpture terrace on the roof, with its wonderful views of the city) and four intermediate levels of halls with large windows looking out over the park onto vistas sectioned by the different levels.

The third body, which connects the other two, unfolds in a large central area of elevator towers with a double-ramp system. The continuous ramps connect the different levels from the top down, giving access to the halls, while the bridge ramps cross the space between the intermediate levels, connecting the office wing and the smaller halls. This complex area of tensions—difficult to construct with a conventional geometry—leads the visitor to discover the space anew in the glimpses of light originating where the dark shadows of the ramps come to an end, in the vista that opens up over the large area above the access to the halls or in the fragmented view of the park.

From the intimate and peaceful interior of the open-air patio of the first museum, the visitor passes to the interior of the contrasted and dynamic space encased and interlinked by the ramps of the new extension. Villanueva believed that "the architect should be a humanist." For him, these two museums in one were, as in the case of the School of Architecture, buildings that he brought to life with his work and in which he "lived" as though they were his own houses.

1 Interior view of the circulation ramps, second
  extension
2 and 3 Detail of the ramps and interior space,
  second extension
4 Last room of the Museum: the open-air terrace
  with panoramic views over the city of Caracas and
  sculptures by Henry Moore in the foreground
5 Double ramp, with skylights, leading to the open-air
  terrace-hall and to the terrace of the other wing

4

5

Venezuelan Pavilion at the Montreal Expo of 1967

Montreal, Canada
1967
Collaborators: Ricardo de Sola
Arthur Erickson
Developer: Government of Venezuela

The Venezuelan Pavilion for the Montreal Expo of 1967 was an exceptional work—one that, despite its seemingly atypical attributes, accurately reflected Villanueva's convictions, ethics, and aesthetics. It was a simple and straightforward design executed with an economy of resources. Fresh and cheerful, synthetic and colorful, it was far removed from the neoclassical Venezuelan Pavilion he designed with Luis Malausena for the 1937 International Exposition in Paris. According to Juan Pedro Posani, Villanueva's pavilion "brings to mind an old sketch by Le Corbusier which the latter used to define scale and its value": a boxlike cube with some dots representing people. Indeed, the pavilion was modeled on the cube as the ideal abstract shape to represent space on any scale. Because of its primary form, it stood out from the cacophony of elaborate pavilions competing for attention at the Expo. Starting from this idea-shape, the program was organized into three areas: an audio-visual presentation of Venezuela, a representation of the jungle, and an area for services and facilities. The scheme evolved from the linear layout of a large cube and two smaller ones to the final design, which was sketched on a napkin and consisted of three alternated cubes of the same size grouped together—in Philip Johnson's view, a true example of minimal art that was illustrative of the youthful and playful qualities that permeated Villanueva's work.

The pavilion was given an excellent location, between one of the canals and the Saint Lawrence River, on a 1,500-square-meter plot of land. On entering the site, the first thing encountered was a large *Stabile* by Calder in the foreground, set off against other small and large sculptures, which make up the building in the background. The three cubes were situated on a concrete platform of sloping planes and ramps, linked together by a circulation and access area covered with a lower roof that offered various changing perspectives. These cubes featured the letters of the word *Venezuela* and were like children's building blocks—small objects materialized in large volumes that alter the conditions of scale and of architectural expression itself. Their poetry lay in their polished sides and corners painted red, blue, green, yellow, black, and orange. These strong, bright colors reflected images in their shadows, repeating themselves and unfolding a palette of harmonies and contrasts. Although they were originally planned to be 15 meters long on each side, they ended up 13 x 13-meter steel structures covered with aluminum sheets designed by engineer Ricardo de Sola, who participated actively in the execution of the project.

One of the cubes consisted of three levels that housed a café, administrative offices, and toilets. The second showed an audio-visual presentation of Venezuela on four screens mounted on the inside walls. In the last, the "natural" representation of the jungle was replaced by a large kinetic sculpture by Jesús Soto consisting of long aluminum bars suspended from the ceiling and reflected in a body of water on the floor. These bars rotated slowly from side to side to the accompaniment of a musical composition called "Cromovibraphony," written for the exposition by the Venezuelan musician Antonio Estévez. In this brightly illuminated white space, Soto's sculpture was, in the words of the artist, "no more than a partial detector of the infinite vibrations that Villanueva's cube delimits in the universe."

1 Preliminary sketch
2 Main access, northwest façade

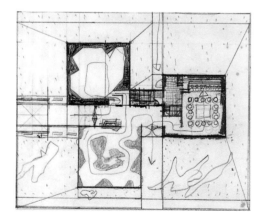

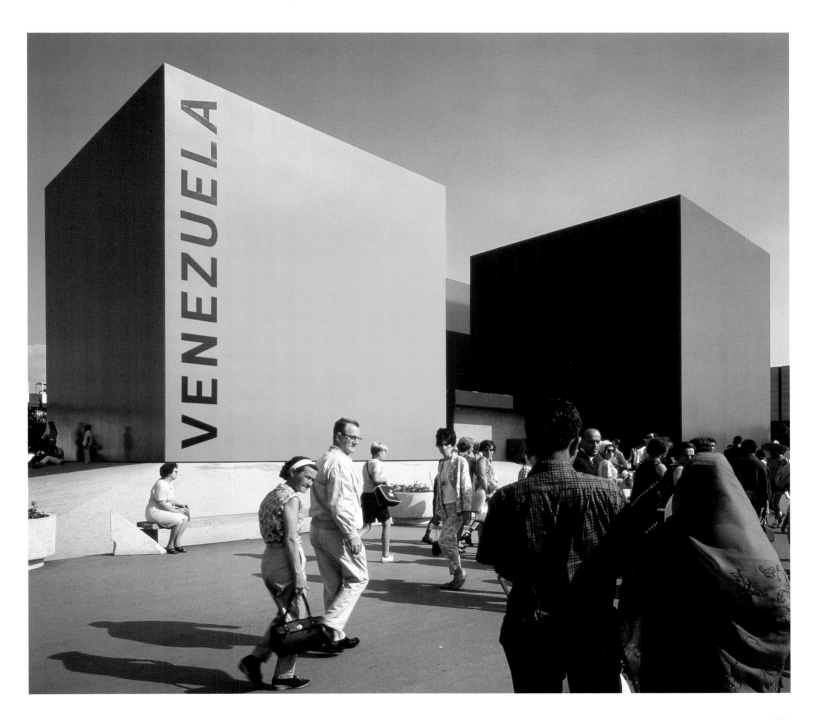

1, 2, and 3 Sketches of the evolution of the idea
4 Section and elevation
5 Ground floor plan
6 Sketch of the draft design
7 Detail of the interior with the Jesús Soto installation

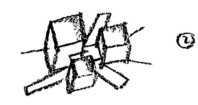

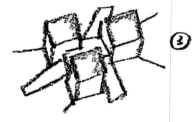

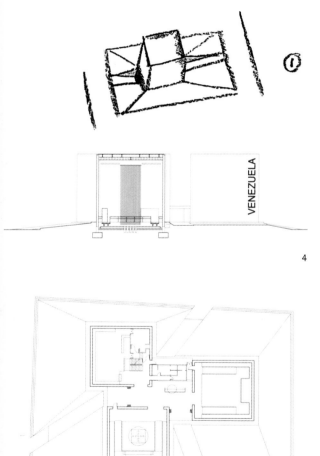

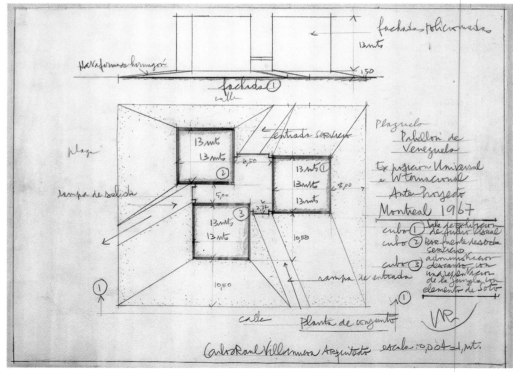

Jesús Soto Museum

Bolívar City, Bolívar State
1970–72
Developer: Corporación Venezolana de Guayana

1 Initial sketches
2 View of the central courtyard to the east

The Jesús Soto Museum of Modern Art, located in Bolívar City (in the south of Venezuela, on the banks of the Orinoco), was Villanueva's last work: a deeply felt homage to his close friend Jesús "The Tiger" Soto and a humble space for an excellent collection of contemporary art. Villanueva designed an appropriate counterpoint for the collection, which included kinetic, geometrical, optical, concrete, and abstract art. The building is a box with small, repeated moveable and adjustable openings, some horizontal and others vertical, some square and others elongated, through which light and vision penetrate. A shifting interplay of lights and shadows is projected, and a torrent of blinding light explodes, annulling the tones and contrasts in the genesis of a space that is presented and constructed almost, in Villanueva's words, "without the need to use materials."

An austere building, it is a work that incorporates resonances and quotations from many of his previous works: the original idea of the first Museum of Fine Arts, the transparency and spatial fluency of Sotavento, the climatic adaptation of the School of Petroleum Engineering in Maracaibo, and the materialization of the cube of the Montreal Expo's Venezuelan Pavilion, among others.

In endless design sketches the museum was projected as a series of buildings, with the blocks of the exhibition halls initially grouped together in a compact wing attached to the cylindrical volume of the cafeteria, which later disappeared. In the end, the halls were organized in a relatively random fashion, circumscribing an irregularly shaped central courtyard, and connecting and communicating with each other through low galleries in which the perforated concrete walls alternate with the openings leading to the outer enclosure. The museum consists of a series of buildings: an entry, a two-story management and administration building, a cement cube that houses Soto's works, and four exhibition areas. One of these cubes occupies two floors; the others are smaller, one floor structures with exterior loggias and moveable, vertical latticed planes. Designed as closed and empty boxes, they are cut through only by a long line of light that enters from a chink between the wall and the ceiling.

The composition's center of gravity is the interior patio—an irregular area articulated by the tense arrangement of the various wings. This space is given over to a garden of sculptures that stand out against the strong presence of the different volumes.

As in the new building for the Museum of Fine Arts, the Jesús Soto Museum was built using prefabricated elements: slabs separate the stories, and prefabricated concrete beams are placed in a vertical position with the ribs facing outward. These, together with the pronounced shadows, form a linear theme against which Soto's kinetic sculptures react.

Villanueva advocated the advance of technology and saw in the industrialization of the construction process the leap that would revolutionize design methods. He believed that to optimize the advantages of prefabricated materials, basic pieces should be neither too small nor too large, so as not to compromise creative freedom. For Villanueva, architecture was "an abstract rather than representational art, but with the function and essence of Cartesian logic."

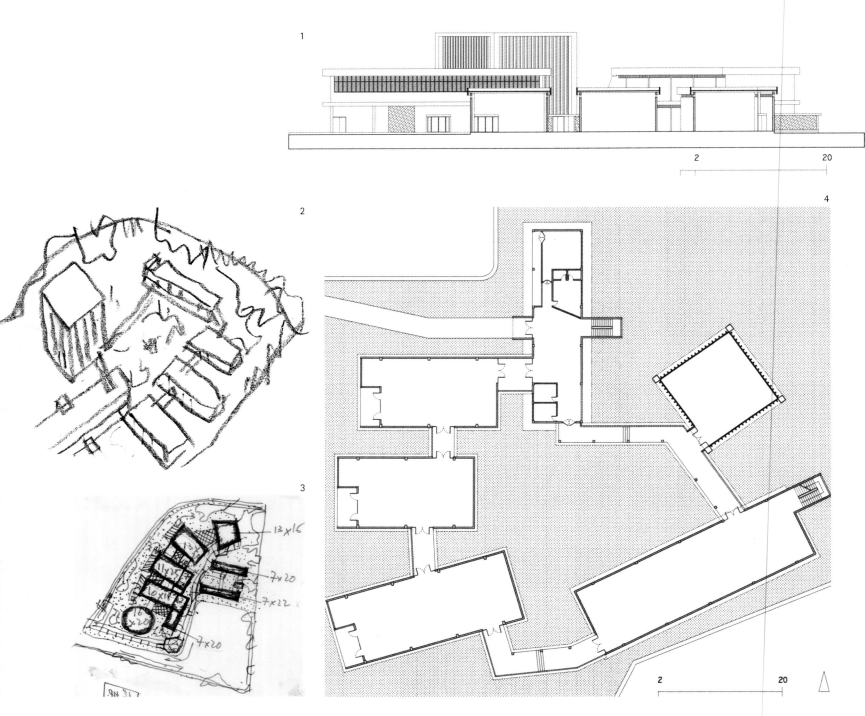

1

2

3

4

13×16

7×20

7×22 ×

7×20

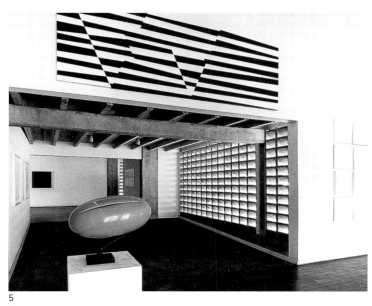

1 Cross section through the exhibition halls, main façade in projection
2 Sketch of the preliminary design
3 Sketch of the first alternatives
4 Ground floor plan
5 Interior view of one of the halls connecting the exhibition halls
6 West façade

5
6

1 View of the central courtyard
2 Interior view of one of the exhibition halls

complete works

1 Florida Club
Residential development La Florida
Caracas, Federal District
1928
Draft design for competition
Not executed

2 Banco Obrero and Banco Agrícola y Pecuario Headquarters
Plaza Girardot
Maracay, Aragua State
1929
Banco Obrero
Modification of a preexisting design by engineer André Potel; currently the Museum of History and Anthropology

3 Jardín Hotel
Plaza Bolívar, Maracay, Aragua State
1929–30
Ministry of Public Works
Remodel of a residential complex during construction; original design by engineer André Potel. Currently the headquarters of the state government
See page 166, photo 9

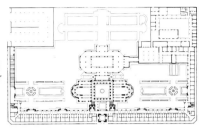

4 Sports Club
Plaza Bolívar
Maracay, Aragua State
1930
Ministry of Public Works
Demolished
See page 162, work 4.1

5 Llanero House
Undated
Ministry of Public Works
Two different designs

6 Plaza Bolívar
Maracay, Aragua State
1930–35
Ministry of Public Works

7 Bullring
Maracay, Aragua State
1931–32
Developer: Gómez Family

8 Bolivarian Museum
Esquina de Pajaritos
Caracas, Federal District
1931–32
Ministry of Public Works

9 Mental Hospital
Lídice
Caracas, Federal District
1931–33
Ministry of Public Works

10 Stables
El Paraíso Racetrack
Caracas, Federal District
1933
Developer: Gonzalo Gómez
Demolished

11 La Macarena House
Collaborator: Luis Malaussena
Residential development Las Delicias
Maracay, Aragua State
1933–35
Developer: Florencio Gómez

12 Private Houses
Twenty-three villas and houses located in the residential developments of La Florida, El Paraíso and La Pastora
Caracas, Federal District
1933–38
Developer: Juan Bernardo Arismendi and others

13 Architect's Private House
Av. Andrés Bello
Residential development La Florida
Caracas, Federal District
1934
Demolished
See page 166, photo 10

14 Plaza Carabobo
Caracas, Federal District
1934
Ministry of Public Works
Fountain and sculptures: Francisco Narváez

15 Museum of Fine Arts
Los Caobos
Caracas, Federal District
1935–38
Ministry of Public Works
Reliefs: Francisco Narváez
See page 130

16 Museum of Natural Sciences
Los Caobos
Caracas, Federal District
1936–39
Ministry of Public Works
Reliefs: Francisco Narváez

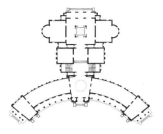

17 Venezuelan Pavilion at the Paris Exposition
Collaborators: Luis Malaussena and André Gutton
Paris, France
1937
Government of Venezuela
Demolished

18 Simón Bolívar Plaza
Valdivia, Valparaíso
Chile
1938
Ministry of Public Works
Design

19 Los Rosales and El Prado Residential Estates
Caracas, Federal District
1938–40
Developer: Juan Bernardo Arismendi

20 Hospital Prototype Designs Type A and Type B
Collaborator for type A: Herman Blasser
1938–40
Ministry of Public Works
Hospital prototype designs for cities in the Venezuelan interior

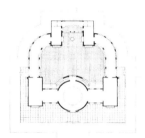

21 Fourteen Private Buildings
Offices, industrial premises, shops and apartment buildings located in El Conde, San Agustín, Los Rosales, Sabana Grande, El Valle and Santa Rosa
Caracas, Federal District
1938–48
Developer: Juan Bernardo Arismendi and others

22 Private Houses
Forty-six private houses and villas located in the residential developments of La Florida, El Paraíso, Sabana Grande and Los Rosales
Caracas, Federal District
1939
Developer: Juan Bernardo Arismendi and others

23 Hospitals
Guanare, Portuguesa State; Araya and Río Caribe, Sucre State; and San Felipe, Yaracuy State
1939–41
Ministry of Public Works
Four hospitals located in different Venezuelan cities. Río Caribe was an extension of an existing building.

24 Gran Colombia School
Caracas, Federal District
1939–42
Ministry of Public Works
Currently the Francisco Pimentel School.
Bas reliefs: Francisco Narváez

25 Headquarters of the Venezuelan Chamber of Engineers
Los Caobos
Caracas, Federal District
1940
Developer: Venezuelan Chamber of Engineers
Competition design, not executed

26 La Concordia Plaza
Quinta Crespo
Caracas, Federal District
1940
Ministry of Public Works
Demolished
See page 167, photo 13

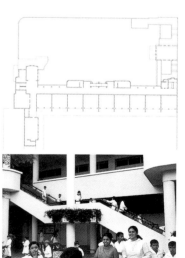

27 Buena Vista Preorientation Boarding School
Collaborator: Herman Blasser
Los Teques, Miranda State
1940–42
Ministry of Public Works
A complex of buildings including school dormitories, lecture rooms, workshops, sports fields, administration and service areas, a church and a plaza. The dormitory building was an adaptation of a preexisting prison building.

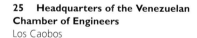

28 Private Houses
Twenty houses and villas located in the residential developments of La Florida, El Paraíso, Sabana Grande and San Juan
Caracas, Federal District
1940–45
Developer: Juan Bernardo Arismendi and others

29 Passenger Terminal
Valera Airport
Trujillo State
1941–42
Ministry of Public Works

30 El Silencio Redevelopment
Caracas, Federal District
1941–45
Banco Obrero
Seven urban blocks with a total of 7,797 apartments and 207 shop premises.
See page 34

31 Venezuela Tuberculosis Clinic
Mérida, Mérida State
1942–45
Ministry of Public Works

32 Radio Communications Building of Venezuela
Caracas, Federal District
1943
Ministry of Public Works

33 General Rafael Urdaneta Development
Maracaibo, Zulia State
1943–47
Banco Obrero
A total of 1,000 houses and 424 apartments, developed for an estimated population of 7,300 persons on 60 hectares, which at the time represented

7 percent of the total area of Maracaibo. The development also included local shopping centres, schools, clinics, sports facilities, parks, and gardens.

34 Unidad Vacacional Los Caracas
Collaborators: Armando Vegas, Martín Vegas
Los Caracas, El Botuco and Río Grande Sectors
Litoral Central
1944
Ministry of Public Works and Ministry of Health and Social Services
Originally the National Leper Hospital, it is currently a workers' resort. The original design included an urban plan and apartment buildings, houses, and service facilities, with approximately 36 different building types, from single-family houses, swimming pools, and clubs to apartment buildings (*see floor plans at right*) linked by a block of community facilities. The buildings for bachelors, the apartment blocks, the hotel, the treatment of the

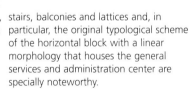

stairs, balconies and lattices and, in particular, the original typological scheme of the horizontal block with a linear morphology that houses the general services and administration center are specially noteworthy.

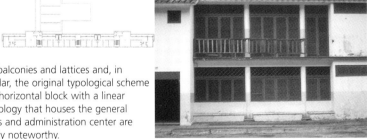

35 University Campus of Caracas
Caracas, Federal District
1944–70
University Campus Institute
Uninterrupted planning and building of the University Campus of Caracas.
See pages 52 and 152

36 Rafael Urdaneta Plaza
El Silencio
Caracas, Federal District
1945
Ministry of Public Works
Currently Plaza O'Leary
Fountains and sculptures: Francisco Narváez

37 University Hospital
Collaborators: Thomas R. Ponton and Edgar Martin
Ciudad Universitaria
Caracas, Federal District
1945
University Campus Institute
Façade polychromy: Mateo Manaure
See page 56

38 Anatomical Institute
Ciudad Universitaria
Caracas, Federal District
1945
University Campus Institute

University Campus of Caracas
(see also pages 151–162)

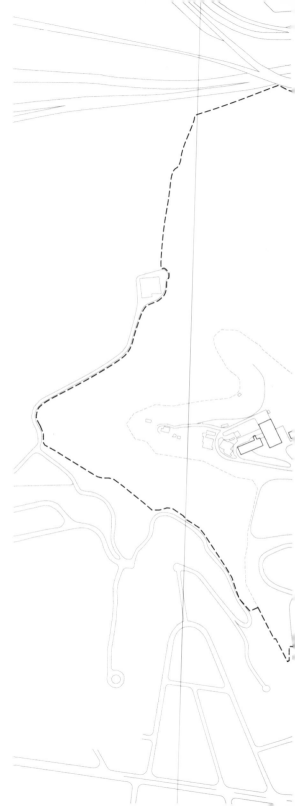

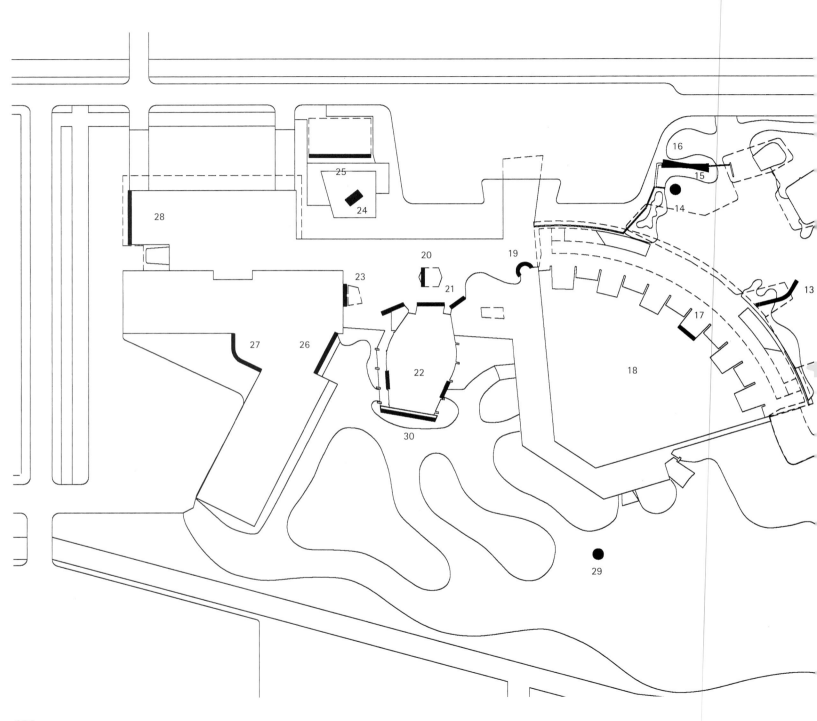

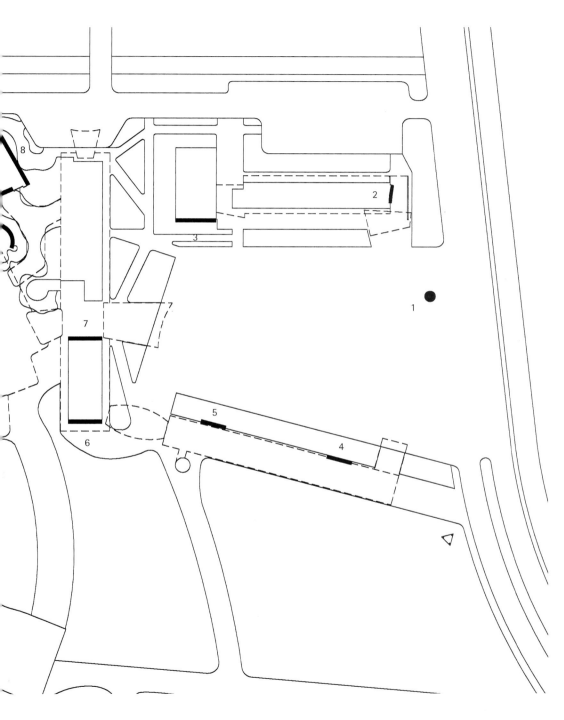

Works of art in the Central Area of the University Campus of Caracas

1 Francisco Narváez, *Sculpture*
2 André Bloc, *Mural in Relief*
3 Oswaldo Vigas, *A Static Element in Five Positions*
4 Armando Barrios, *Mural*
5 Oswaldo Vigas, *Static Composition – Dynamic Composition*
6 Oswaldo Vigas, *An Element – Treble Character*
7 Oswaldo Vigas, *Vertical Character in Horizontal Evolution*
8 Mateo Manaure, *Mural*
9 Mateo Manaure, *Stained-glass Window*
10 Pascual Navarro, *Mural*
11 Henri Laurens, *Amphion*
12 Fernand Léger, *Bimural*
13 Victor Vasarély, *Homage to Malevich*
14 Jean Arp, *Cloud Shepherd*
15 Mateo Manaure, *Mural*
16 Mateo Manaure, *Mural*
17 Carlos González Bogen, *Mural*
18 Alexander Calder, *Stabile*
19 Mateo Manaure, *Mural*
20 Victor Vasarély, *Positive and Negative*
21 Pascual Navarro, *Mural*
22 Mateo Manaure, *Acoustic Complements*
23 Mateo Manaure, *Mural*
24 Antoine Pevsner, *Dynamism at 30 Degrees*
25 Victor Vasarély, *Sophia*
26 Fernand Léger, *Stained-glass Window*
27 Carlos González Bogen, *Mural*
28 Pascual Navarro, *Mural*
29 Baltazar Lobo, *Maternity*
30 Mateo Manaure, *Mural*

39 Institute of Experimental Medicine
Ciudad Universitaria
Caracas, Federal District
1945
University Campus Institute
On the left of the photograph

40 Institute of Anatomical and Pathological Medicine
Ciudad Universitaria
Caracas, Federal District
1945
University Campus Institute
On the right of the photograph

41 Luis Razetti Cancer Institute
Ciudad Universitaria
Caracas, Federal District
1945
University Campus Institute
Not executed

42 Rafael Urdaneta School
Unidad Vecinal General Rafael Urdaneta
Maracaibo, Zulia State
1945–46
Ministry of Public Works

43 San Martín Cooperative Housing
Avenida San Martín
Caracas, Federal District
1945–49
Banco Obrero
One 8-story block with 150 apartments and three 4-story blocks with a total of 168 apartments.

44 El Hipódromo Development
Collaborator: Carlos Celis
Maracay, Aragua State
1946
Banco Obrero

45 Nursing School Lecture Room Building and Dormitories
Ciudad Universitaria
Caracas, Federal District
1946
University Campus Institute
Polychromy: Braulio Salazar

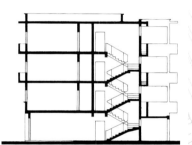

46 Neighborhood Unit Los Morichales
Ciudad Bolívar, Bolívar State
1947
Banco Obrero

47 Urdaneta Development
Collaborator: Leopoldo Martínez
Catia
Caracas, Federal District
1947–48, 1950, 1957
Banco Obrero
The development originally consisted of 276 houses (three different building types) built in 1948, but construction

continued during the following years: 973 houses were built from 1950 to 1953, and during the last stage 164 apartments were built in 4- and 5-story blocks from 1956 to 1957.

48 Industrial Technical High School
Ciudad Universitaria
Caracas, Federal District
1948
University Campus Institute
Workshop mural: Mateo Manaure
(see photograph on the right)

49 Botanical Institute
Ciudad Universitaria
Caracas, Federal District
1948
University Campus Institute

50 Rental Area Residential Unit
Zona Rental, Ciudad Universitaria
Caracas, Federal District
1948
University Campus Institute
Not executed

51 Francisco de Miranda Cooperative Housing Unit
Casalta, Caracas, Federal District
1948
Banco Obrero
Twenty-nine blocks with ninety-six 4-story buildings, totalling 768 apartments, including play areas, parks, and parking lots. See page 167, photo 16

52 Coronel Delgado Chalbaud Neighborhood Unit
Coche
Caracas, Federal District
1948–50
Banco Obrero
A total of 250 worker houses, 307 intermediate-level houses, 552 middle-class houses and 415 apartments in 4-story buildings, totalling 1,525 dwellings with common facilities: shopping area, sports facilities, schools, civic and health center, gardens, and parking lots
See page 167, photo 17

53 Los Medanos Neighborhood Unit
Collaborators: Carlos Celis, Carlos Brando, and Víctor Mantilla
Coro, Falcón State
1948–52
Banco Obrero
A neighborhood with 594 dwellings.

54 Las Delicias Neighborhood Unit
Collaborator: Carlos Celis
Maracay, Aragua State
1948–52
Banco Obrero
A neighborhood with 1,317 dwellings for a population of 7,902 inhabitants

55 Student Residence Halls
Ciudad Universitaria
Caracas, Federal District
1949
University Campus Institute
A complex of four buildings

56 Houses for Directors
Ciudad Universitaria
Caracas, Federal District
1949
University Campus Institute
Not executed

57 Laboratory of Testing Materials
Ciudad Universitaria
Caracas, Federal District
1949
University Campus Institute

58 Laboratory of Petroleum, Chemistry and Geology
Ciudad Universitaria
Caracas, Federal District
1949
University Campus Institute

59 Cafeteria and Shop
Ciudad Universitaria
Caracas, Federal District
1949–50
University Campus Institute
Later turned into a University canteen, partly demolished

60 Institute of Tropical Medicine
Ciudad Universitaria
Caracas, Federal District
1949-1950
University Campus Institute

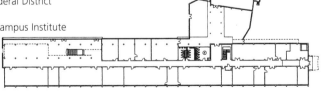

61 Olympic Stadium
Ciudad Universitaria
Caracas, Federal District
1949–50
University Campus Institute
See page 60

62 Baseball Stadium
Ciudad Universitaria
Caracas, Federal District
1949–50
University Campus Institute
See page 60

63 Tennis Courts
Ciudad Universitaria
Caracas, Federal District
1949–50
University Campus Institute

64 Extension to the Museum of Natural Sciences
Los Caobos
Caracas, Federal District
1950
Ministry of Public Works

65 Shopping Centre
Collaborator: Carlos Celis
Unidad Vecinal Coronel Delgado
Chalbaud, Coche
Caracas, Federal District
1950
Banco Obrero

66 School of Engineering
Ciudad Universitaria
Caracas, Federal District
1950
University Campus Institute
Polychromy on library façade:
Alejandro Otero

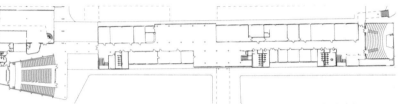

67 Laboratory of Hydraulics
Ciudad Universitaria
Caracas, Federal District
1950
University Campus Institute

68 Laboratory of Physics and Mathematics
Ciudad Universitaria
Caracas, Federal District
1950
University Campus Institute

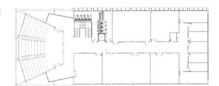

69 Biology Laboratory
Ciudad Universitaria
Caracas, Federal District
1950–52
University Campus Institute

70 Ciudad Tablitas Redevelopment
Collaborator: Carlos Celis
Caracas, Federal District
1950–53
Banco Obrero
A series of 4-story buildings with a total
of 976 apartments

71 Covered Walkways
Ciudad Universitaria
Caracas, Federal District
1950–59
University Campus Institute
Executed in stages: School of
Engineering (1950–54); Central Area
(1952–53), Architecture and Pharmacy
(1957–59). See pages 86–87

72 Quinta Crespo Housing Estate
Collaborator: Carlos Celis
Quinta Crespo
Caracas, Federal District
1951
Banco Obrero
Not executed

73 Caoma House
Residential development La Florida
Caracas, Federal District
1951–52
Architect's private town house.
See page 20

74 Parish House
Ciudad Universitaria
Caracas, Federal District
1952
University Campus Institute
Not executed

75 Nursing School Service and Administration Building
Ciudad Universitaria
Caracas, Federal District
1952
University Campus Institute

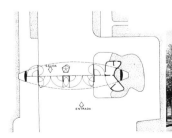

92 Hacienda La Pimpera House
Barlovento, Miranda State
1954
Developer: Angel Ugueto

93 Lomas de Pro Patria Development
Collaborators: Guido Bermúdez and Carlos Brando
Pro Patria, Caracas, Federal District
1954
Banco Obrero (Cerro Piloto Plan)
Twelve 15-story superblocks with 1,819 apartments in Lomas de Pro Patria and

four 4-story blocks with 88 apartments in Brisas de Pro Patria

94 Altos de Cutira Residential Estate
Collaborators: Guido Bermúdez and Carlos Brando
Caracas, Federal District
1954
Banco Obrero (Cerro Piloto Plan)
Two 15-story superblocks and seven 4-story blocks

95 Diego de Losada Development
Collaborators: Guido Bermúdez and Carlos Brando
Caracas, Federal District
1954
Banco Obrero
Two 15- and 11-story superblocks and fifteen 4-story blocks. It formed part of the Cerro Piloto Plan.

96 Cotiza Housing Estate
Collaborators: Guido Bermúdez and Carlos Brando
Caracas, Federal District
1954
Banco Obrero
One 15-story superblock and community facilities. It formed part of the Cerro Piloto Plan.

97 Lomas de Urdaneta Development
Collaborators: Guido Bermúdez and Carlos Brando
Caracas, Federal District
1954–55
Banco Obrero (Cerro Piloto Plan)
Twelve 15-story superblocks with a total of 1,990 apartments

98 Atlántico Norte Development
Collaborators: Guido Bermúdez and Carlos Brando
Caracas, Federal District
1954–55
Banco Obrero
Five 15-story superblocks, a duplex superblock and a 4-story block. It formed part of the Cerro Piloto Plan.

99 Artigas Residential Estate
Collaborators: Guido Bermúdez and Carlos Brando
Caracas, Federal District
1954–55
Banco Obrero
Three 15-story superblocks and six 4-story blocks. It formed part of the Cerro Piloto Plan.

100 Insectary of the Institute of Hygiene
Ciudad Universitaria
Caracas, Federal District
1954–56
University Campus Institute

101 School of Architecture
Ciudad Universitaria
Caracas, Federal District
1954–56
University Campus Institute
Façade polychromy: Alejandro Otero
See page 112

102 Church for the University Campus
Ciudad Universitaria
Caracas, Federal District
1955
University Campus Institute
Draft design
See page 170, photo 33

103 La Vega Residential Estate
Collaborators: Guido Bermúdez and Carlos Brando
Caracas, Federal District
1955
Banco Obrero
Two 15-story superblocks and one 4-story block. The complex formed part of the Cerro Piloto Plan.

104 23 de Enero Development
[First Stage]
Collaborators: Carlos Brando and José Manuel Mijares
Caracas, Federal District
1955
Banco Obrero
Formerly 2 de Diciembre Development.
See page 44

105 Rental Area Building
Ciudad Universitaria
Caracas, Federal District
1955–57
University Campus Institute
Two versions, neither executed

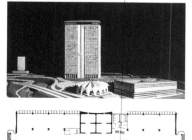

106 Simón Rodríguez Development
Collaborator: José Manuel Mijares
Caracas, Federal District
1956
Banco Obrero
Eight 15-story superblocks with a total of 1,380 apartments and community facilities

107   23 de Enero Development
[Second Stage]
Collaborators: José Hoffman and José
Manuel Mijares
Caracas, Federal District
1956
Banco Obrero
See page 44

108   School of Pharmacy
Ciudad Universitaria
Caracas, Federal District
1956–57
University Campus Institute
Façade polychromy: Alejandro Otero

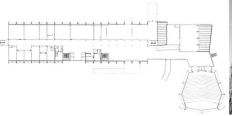

**109   School of Petroleum
Engineering**
Universidad del Zulia
Maracaibo, Zulia State
1956–57
Part of Zulia University
See page 126

110   School of Dentistry
Ciudad Universitaria
Caracas, Federal District
1957
University Campus Institute
Façade polychromy: Omar Carreño
See page 120

111   23 de Enero Development
[Third Stage]
Collaborator: José M. Mijares
Caracas, Federal District
1957
Banco Obrero
See page 44

112   Chapel of La Asunción
Collaborator: Juan Pedro Posani
Residential development 23 de Enero
Caracas, Federal District
1957
Banco Obrero
See page 51

113   Sotavento House
Residential development Palmar Este
Caraballeda, Vargas State
1957–58
Architect's beach house
See page 28

114   Covered Gymnasium
Ciudad Universitaria
Caracas, Federal District
1958
University Campus Institute
The concrete roof was never built.

**115   Swimming Pool Complex,
Training Gymnasium and Sports
Department**
Ciudad Universitaria
Caracas, Federal District
1958–59
University Campus Institute
See page 66

116   Nacional Building
Collaborator: Juan Pedro Posani
Maracaibo, Zulia State
1960
Ministry of Public Works
Draft design

117   La Salle Foundation
Maripérez
Caracas, Federal District
1961–62
Developer: La Salle
Foundation

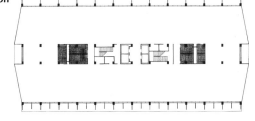

118   Caomita House
El Pedregal
Caracas, Federal District
1962
Private town house belonging to the
architect's son, Francisco Villanueva

**119   Tropical and Experimental
Medicine Laboratories**
Ciudad Universitaria
Caracas, Federal District
1962–64
University Campus Institute

**120   Institute of Materials and
Structural Models**
Ciudad Universitaria
Caracas, Federal District
1962–64
Planning direction: Central University of
Venezuela (UCV)

121   Los Cedros House
Country Club
Caracas, Federal District
1963–64
Developer: Angel Ugueto

122 Law School
Ciudad Universitaria
Caracas, Federal District
1963–67
Planning direction: UCV
Not executed

123 School of Sciences
Collaborator: Gorka Dorronsoro
Ciudad Universitaria
Caracas, Federal District
1963–67
Planning direction: UCV
Not executed

124 Laboratory of Marine Science
Ciudad Universitaria
Caracas, Federal District
1963–67
Planning direction: UCV
Draft design

125 School of Economics
Collaborators: Gorka Dorronsoro and
Juan Pedro Posani
Ciudad Universitaria
Caracas, Federal District
1963–67
Planning direction: UCV
See page 171, photo 39

126 School of Sanitary Engineering
Collaborator: Gorka Dorronsoro
Ciudad Universitaria
Caracas, Federal District
1963–67
Planning direction: UCV
See page 172, photo 42

127 School of Industrial Engineering
Collaborator: Gorka Dorronsoro
Ciudad Universitaria
Caracas, Federal District
1963–67
Planning direction: UCV
Not executed

128 Plaza Estrella Building
Collaborators: Oscar Carmona
and Gerónimo Puig
Residential development San
Bernardino
Caracas, Federal District
1964
Family commission

129 House for Alejandro Otero
San Antonio de los Altos
1965
Developer: Alejandro Otero
Draft design

130 Museum of Fine Arts Second Extension
Collaborator: Oscar Carmona
Los Caobos, Federal District, Caracas
1966–76
Ministry of Urban Development
See page 130

131 Venezuelan Pavilion for the Montreal Expo
Collaborators: Ricardo de Sola and
Arthur Erickson
Montreal, Canada
1967
Government of Venezuela
Demolished
See page 138

132 Student Residence
Collaborator: Juan Pedro Posani
Paris University Campus
1969
Developer: Fina Gómez Foundation
Draft design

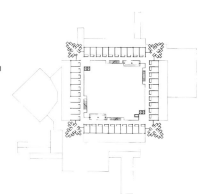

133 House for Clara Rosa Otero
Residential development Tanaguarena
Litoral Central, Vargas State
1969
Developer: Clara Rosa Otero

134 Jesús Soto Museum
Ciudad Bolívar, Bolívar State
1970
Corporación Venezolana de Guayana
See page 142

4.1 Cavalry Barracks
Maracay, Aragua State
1930
Documented by Paulina Villanueva after
having closed this edition

A large group of professionals–architects and engineers, artists and technicians–collaborated with Villanueva during the planning and building stages of many of these works. Naming them all is beyond the scope of this book. Hence, only his most immediate collaborators in certain designs are mentioned in this list of complete works.

Detail of the ceiling, School of Sanitary Engineering,
University Campus of Caracas

biography and chronology

Eighteenth to Nineteenth Century

The Villanueva family, originally from Valencia, Spain, moves to Venezuela in the eighteenth century. By 1816 it owns vast estates and is involved in cattle farming in the San Carlos area of Cojedes State. Dr. Laureano Villanueva, Carlos Raúl's grandfather, is active in politics and the arts, an orator in parliament and the academies, editor, satirical journalist, and author of various works on the history of Venezuela. He holds such posts as rector of the Central University and provisional president of the republic in 1887. His son, Carlos Antonio, leads a distinguished diplomatic career. Venezuela's commissioner at the Paris Expo of 1889, he lives in Europe from then on. He holds the post of Venezuelan Consul in London and researches the history of South American independence. His wife, Paulina Astoul, comes from a Basque family based first in Argentina and then in France.

Venezuela was a colony of Spain from the fifteenth century (Columbus arrived in 1498, on his third voyage). Caracas, founded in 1567 by Diego Losada, became a focal point in the struggle for colonial independence. The country is sparsely populated and has an agricultural economy based on coffee and cocoa.

1900
Carlos Raúl is born in London on May 30, son of Carlos Antonio Villanueva and Paulina Astoul. Shortly afterwards the family moves to France. He is brought up in a European diplomatic atmosphere and receives his early education from the Lycee Condorcet in Paris. Between 1918 and 1919 he spends a long period in Málaga, returning later to Paris.

Caracas has a population of 70,000, mostly living in one-floor houses with red-tiled roofs. In 1908 General Juan V. Gómez starts his dictatorship.

1920–28
He studies architecture at the Ecole des Beaux Arts in Paris, in Gabriel Héraud's studio, where his older brother, Marcel, had also studied.

Stalin rises to power.

In the 1920s, petroleum extraction by American, English, and Dutch companies

under the fiscal control of the government brings about radical changes in the country's economic, social, and cultural structures.

Alejandro Chataing, the architect whose eclectic style put its stamp on Caracas in the first part of the century, dies.

In the 1930s the dominant architecture among the new middle class follows Hispanic lines (neocolonial and other historic styles such as the Basque style and the neobaroque), while examples of the modern movement appear.

1927
During his years as a student he carries out several projects independently of the school, among them a zoo in Nicaragua (his father is minister-ambassador in Nicaragua at this time) and a club in Costa Rica. He works with Léon Joseph Madeline in Paris.

1928
He participates as an assistant to a fellow student at Héraud's studio, Roger-Léopold Hummel, on the project *Un hôtel d'ambassade à construire dans un grand pays d'Extreme Orient*, winner of the Deuxième Grand Prix. On June 6 he graduates from the Ecole des Beaux Arts in Paris. He travels to Venezuela for the first time and then to the United States, where he works until the following year with his brother Marcel.

1929
He returns to Venezuela and begins to work in the Ministry of Public Works, where he serves as the Director of Building and Ornamental Works until 1939. From the start he knows how to adapt his Paris training to prevailing geopolitical conditions in Venezuela. The process is carried out by rehearsing an aesthetic pattern that over time becomes increasingly abstract, universal, and accepted.

1930
On the centenary of Bolívar's death the government commissions an extensive plan of public works in Maracay. The Jardín Hotel is inaugurated on December 19.

Le Corbusier designs the Villa Stein, Garches, Paris; Konstantin Melnikov, the Rusakov Workers' Club, Moscow. First talkie: *The Jazz Singer*.

The seven largest oil companies establish a cartel of international prices. The first CIAM is held in La Sarraz (Switzerland), with Siegfried Giedion as secretary. Eugène Freyssinet invents prestressed concrete.

The outset of the Great Depression. The Museum of Modern Art opens in New York. Mies van der Rohe designs the German Pavilion, Barcelona. García Lorca writes *A Poet in New York*.

Pluto is discovered. Nylon invented.

1932–33
The Maracay Bullring is built and inaugurated in 1933. On January 28 Villanueva marries Margot Arismendi and they remain together until his death. He takes over the third chair in the Academy of Physics, Mathematics, and Natural Sciences.
1934
Villanueva builds his first house in La Florida. The Plaza Carabobo is inaugurated, with works by the sculptor Francisco Narváez, with whom Villanueva establishes a long and fruitful working relationship.
1935
Building work begins on the Museum of Fine Arts in Los Caobos, Caracas.
1936
On July 24 his French degree in architecture is ratified in Venezuela.
1937
Together with Luis Malaussena, Villanueva executes the Venezuelan Pavilion at the International Exposition in Paris. The theme of the integration of the arts stands out in many of the pavilions at the exposition, particularly the Finish pavilion by Alvar Aalto and José Luis Sert's and Luis Lacasa's Republic of Spain's pavilion, with works by Pablo Picasso, Julio González, Alberto Sánchez, Joán Miró, and Alexander Calder. Pompous, overbearing pavilions for Nazi Germany and the Soviet Union mar the fair. Villanueva remains in Paris for seven months (1937–38), where he studies at the Institute of Town Planning at the University of Paris.

General López Contreras succeeds Gómez as president, and a new stage of political openness and modernization begins. Caracas renovates its traditional center, with an emphasis on urban expansion and modern residential development (the metropolitan area grows to 250,000 inhabitants); an ideal setting for new trends in architecture and town planning.

Roosevelt is president of the United States. Nazis make major gains in the Reichstag. Hitler closes the Bauhaus school and bans modern art. Calder designs mobile sculptures.

Mao Tse-tung starts the Long March.

The civil war breaks out in Spain.

Frank Lloyd Wright designs Fallingwater. Picasso paints *Guernica*.

1938
The Museum of Fine Arts is inaugurated in Caracas. The Committee for Town Planning is created, and is placed under the aegis of the government of the Federal District. It is made up of Villanueva, Carlos Guinand, Enrique García Maldonado, and Gustavo Wallis. Five urban planners serve as consultants. The Caracas Plan is presented, drawn up by a team led by Maurice Rotival, with whom Villanueva is to maintain a strong and lasting friendship. Villanueva is a member of the Society of Architects of Fine Arts in Paris.
1939
The Museum of Natural Sciences is inaugurated in Caracas. Villanueva designs the Gran Columbia School, the first modern school in Venezuela; Francisco Nárvaez executes a relief for the main façade.
1940
Villanueva participates in the Competition for the Headquarters of the Venezuelan Chamber of Engineers, which is won by Luis Eduardo Chataing. He designs the Plaza de la Concordia, built after the demolition of the Rotunda, the old prison of the Gómez regime. He also begins to work at the Banco Obrero, dealing with the implementation of solutions to improve working-class housing.
1941
The government organizes a competition between Villanueva and Guinand for the redevelopment of the El Silencio neighborhood. He is made founding professor of

The end of López Contreras's mandate. General Medina Angarita takes over as

The Mexican oil industry nationalized. Gropius builds the Gropius House, Lincoln, Massachusetts. Lewis Mumford writes *The Culture of Cities*. Research on the first electronic calculator is undertaken. Color TV invented.

The Spanish civil war ends and Franco's dictatorship begins. World War II begins.

Germany, Italy, and Japan form the Axis. Pétain establishes a pro-Nazi government in Vichy, France. Paul Klee dies. Orson Welles directs *Citizen Kane*.

Hitler invades the U.S.S.R. Japan attacks Pearl Harbor. The United States declares president, leading one of the more democratic governments in Venezuela's history: extensive political openness; changes in government structure; the beginning of large economic, social, educational, sanitary, and urban development programs. The metropolitan population of Caracas rises to about 350,000.

The Caracas–La Guaira motorway is designed to connect the capital to the port and the main airport across an uneven terrain with a 900-meter drop in altitude.

General Medina Angarita is overthrown

the School of Architecture (FAU) of the Central University of Venezuela (UCV), created that year, with other professors including Luis Malaussena, Fernando Salvador, and Cipriano Domínguez. He directs one of the composition studios and holds the chairs of town planning and history of architecture. He is corresponding member of the Colombian Society of Architects.

1942
He wins the competition for the Redevelopment of El Silencio. The Gran Colombia School is inaugurated. He becomes a founding member of the Venezuelan Association of Friends of Colonial Art.

1943
The University Campus Institute is created and the Hacienda Ibarra bought to build the campus of Caracas. Villanueva designs the General Rafael Urdaneta Development in Maracaibo, the largest of the projects built by the Banco Obrero.

1944
Blocks 5, 6, and 7 of El Silencio are inaugurated. Villanueva participates in the mission sent by the University Campus Institute to Bogota to carry out a study and draw up a report for the University Campus. Villanueva makes the first joint proposal for the campus and work begins with the preparation of the terrain and the construction of the main access bridge.

1945
Blocks 3 and 4 of El Silencio are inaugurated and, following that, the final stage of

war on Germany and Japan. Alvar Aalto builds the Villa Mairea, Noormarkku, Finland. Giedion publishes *Space, Time, and Architecture*. James Joyce dies.

Enrico Fermi leads a team building the first nuclear reactor, which leads to the atomic bomb.

Patrick Abercrombie draws up the London plan. Oscar Niemeyer designs the restaurant in Pampulha, Brazil.

The Bretton Woods agreement sets up a new international economic order. Allied troops land in Normandy. Jose Luis Sert publishes *Can Our Cities Survive?* Piet Mondrian and Wassily Kandinsky die.

The United States drops the first atomic

by a group of young army officers in alliance with Democratic Action (AD), a political party of the opposition. A new political class speeds up change: a new constitution, wider education, and an ambitious popular housing plan.

Venezuela becomes one of the world's primary producers and exporters of petroleum. The exodus from the interior of the country to Caracas starts covering the hills with shantytowns.

Domínguez begins the design of the Simón Bolívar Center, Caracas's new city center. Arturo Uslar Pietri writes *The Road to El Dorado*.

this residential development, Blocks 1 and 2, and the Plaza Urdaneta, now Plaza O'Leary, with fountains and sculptures by Francisco Narváez. Villanueva designs the buildings of the medical area of the University Campus and begins construction of the Hospital, the Anatomical-Pathological Institute, and the Institute of Experimental Medicine. He is founding member and first president of the Society of Venezuelan Architects and founding member of the National Committee for the Conservation and Protection of the Historic and Cultural Heritage of the Nation. He receives the Order of the Liberator, with the rank of officer, and the Order of Francisco de Miranda.

1946
The Architecture Studio of the Banco Obrero (TABO), consisting of six architects, is set up and Villanueva is nominated consultant architect, responsible for the design of several housing estates in the interior of the country; the construction of four of the estates begins. He is founding director and member of the National Town Planning Commission.

1947
The Banco Obrero begins work on twenty-two residential developments, among them the Urdaneta Development in the Federal District and Los Morichales in Bolívar State, both by Villanueva. At the exhibition of the Pan-American Congress of Architects in Lima he receives a Prize of Honor and a diploma for the University Campus of Caracas. He is nominated honorary member of Peru's Institute of Town Planning.

bombs on Hiroshima and Nagasaki. Japan surrenders. Mussolini is shot. Hitler commits suicide. World War II ends (40 million victims). The United Nations is established. Luis Barragán plans the El Pedregal project for Mexico City.

Le Corbusier writes *Principles of Urbanism*. The bikini is invented.

The United States launches the Marshall Plan to help European countries, excluding Spain. Barragán designs the Barragán house in Mexico City. Albert Camus publishes *The Plague*.

Rómulo Gallegos, the first president to be elected by popular vote (1947), is ousted in a military coup leading to a ten-year dictatorship. Francisco Narváez receives the National Prize for painting.

The Alejandro Otero exhibition *Las cafeteras,* in the Museum of Fine Arts, asserts abstract painting in the country for the first time. Gallegos writes *Tales of Venezuela.*

Baseball player Chico Carrasquel becomes

1948
The Banco Obrero begins work on nine developments and Villanueva designs the Francisco de Miranda and Coronel Delgado Chalbaud Residential Units. He is named corresponding member of the French Society of Town Planners. Auguste Perret dedicates his book, *Contribution à une Theorie de l'Architecture*, to Villanueva. He receives the Medal of Merit from the Creole Petroleum Corporation and, on August 27, the French Legion of Honor.

1949
The first class graduates from the Caracas School of Architecture. Juan-Pedro Posani meets Villanueva and begins a long professional and personal relationship with him. Villanueva designs several schools, student residences, and the Olympic and Baseball Stadiums on the campus, introducing the first significant changes into the campus plan. The Banco Obrero begins work on eleven estates, among them that of San Martín in the Federal District, designed by Villanueva.

1950
The Baseball and Olympic Stadiums are built. He designs the Francisco de Miranda Residential Unit in Casalta for the Banco Obrero. He publishes his book, *Caracas of Yesterday and Today* in Paris. He attends the Congress of Architects in Havana and meets Wifredo Lam.

1951
The Olympic and Baseball Stadiums are inaugurated. The National Housing Plan is

The Cold War begins. Venezuela decrees that 50 percent of oil proceeds go to the state and 50 percent to the oil industry. Mies van der Rohe designs the Lake Shore Drive Apartments in Chicago.

Mao proclaims the People's Republic of China. Germany is divided into two states. The Copenhagen Plan is developed. Simone de Beauvoir writes *The Second Sex.*

The Korean War begins. Diner's Club card appears. Pablo Neruda writes *Cántico general.*

The first European Community is estab-

a national hero. The precise source of the River Orinoco is discovered.

Marcos Pérez Jiménez, member of the military junta, assumes power with the support of the armed forces. With the slogan "A New National Ideal," he modernizes the country, introducing an intensive national plan of public works. *Integral*, the magazine on architecture and the integration of the arts, appears. National television begins broadcasting.

drawn up with the Banco Obrero to be executed by the TABO Architecture Studio: 12,185 new dwellings are planned over four years. Work on ten developments begins, among them Villanueva's and Celis Cepero's Ciudad Tablitas redevelopment. From 1951–52 he designs and builds his second house, Caoma, in the residential estate of La Florida, Caracas. He chairs the Federal District Commission responsible for drawing up the New Decree on Architecture and Town Planning. Villanueva organizes the exhibition *Architecture and Contemporary French Techniques* in the Museum of Fine Arts. José Luis Sert visits Caracas, and through him Villanueva meets Alexander Calder on a trip to the United States at his house in Roxbury, Connecticut.

1952
Between 1952 and 1953 he designs the Central Area of the campus, in which particular importance is given to the "Synthesis of the Arts" project. Construction begins, marking a radical change in the initial plan. The Banco Obrero begins work on five projects, among them the Coronel Delgado Chalbaud Neighborhood Unit by Villanueva. Together with Celis Cepero, he publishes *Popular Housing in Venezuela*. At the Pan-American Congress of Architects in Mexico he gives a conference on the University Campus. He is made corresponding member of the American Institute of Architects. Calder designs the *Flying Saucers* acoustic panels for the Aula Magna Hall. Villanueva's former fellow students from the Ecole des Beaux Arts pay tribute to him in Paris.

lished. Le Corbusier starts work on the Chandigarh Parliament. Sert writes *The Heart of the City*. Jackson Pollock leads abstract expressionism. BBC broadcasts color TV.

Elizabeth II is crowned Queen of England. Aalto builds the Säynätsalo Town Hall. SOM builds the Lever House Building, New York. Arne Jacobsen designs the Ant chair. Calder receives the Grand Prix for sculpture at the Venice Biennial. Ernest Hemingway writes *The Old Man and the Sea.*

1953

Igor Stravinsky directs the Venezuelan Symphonic Orchestra. The Spanish bull-fighter Luis Miguel Domínguín is badly injured in Caracas and retires. Intensive campaign of roadbuilding across the country. The Tamanaco Hotel opens, a symbol of modern leisure and luxury.

The buildings of the Central Area and a large part of the Covered Walkways are inaugurated. The Banco Obrero begins work on seven developments, among them the El Paraiso Unit by Villanueva and Celis Cepero, and the Los Sauces Develop-ment by Villanueva, Guido Bermúdez, and Carlos Brando. The first extension of the Museum of Fine Arts is inaugurated. He establishes the magazine *A, Hombre y Expresión*, together with Posani and Ramón Lozada. In Paris the following works are executed for the Caracas campus: the sculptures *Cloud Shepherd* by Jean Arp, *Amphion* by Henri Laurens, *Maternity* by Balthazar Lobo, and *Dynamism at 30 Degrees* by Antoine Pevsner; the stained-glass windows and mural elements by Fernand Léger; the murals by Oswaldo Vigas and André Bloc; and the Victor Vasarély works *Homage to Malevich*, *Positive-Negative,* and *Sophia*. The works are exhibited in the Musée National d'Art Moderne in Paris and sent to Caracas the following year. Calder executes the *Snowstorm* mobile, which is installed today in the School of Architecture and Town Planning.

The Korean War ends. An agreement to establish U.S. military bases in Spain puts an end to Spain's international isolation. Stalin dies. Le Corbusier builds the Unité d'Habitation, Marseille; Eero Saarinen builds the MIT Chapel, Cambridge, Massachusetts. José Luis Sert becomes dean of the Harvard Graduate School of Design. Bich designs the first disposable ballpoint pen. Crick and Watson discover the double helix structure of DNA.

1954

The Towers of the Simón Bolívar Center are inaugurated and work begins on the Angloven building and the Mercantile Bank, by Vegas and Galia, and the Electric Company building, by Sanabria.

Aula Magna Hall is inaugurated with the tenth Inter-American Conference. The Hospital and other buildings are also inaugurated, and a large number of the works in the "Synthesis of the Arts" project are put in place. Jean Arp sends Villanueva a model for one of the mosaics that Sophie Taeuber-Arp had executed for the Café Aubert in Strasbourg in 1926; this piece is reproduced in the School of Humanities.

The U.S. Supreme Court rules that seg-regation in schools is unconstitutional. Le Corbusier builds the Chapel at Ronchamp. Mies van der Rohe builds the Seagram Building in New York.

Gio Ponti and Richard Neutra arrive to prepare projects. Christian Dior opens a shop in the capital. Uslar Pietri writes *The Clouds*.

Antoine Pevsner receives the highest distinction in the Triennial of Milan with another copy of the sculpture *Dynamism at 30 Degrees*. In the Banco Obrero, Villanueva, Brando, Bermúdez, and Centella carry out the Cerro Piloto Plan. Work on twenty-one developments starts, including the construction of the superblocks devised in the plan: one of them is built in the record time of forty-two days. Sert gives a series of conferences at the TABO during his visit to present the project for the La Pomona housing estate in Maracaibo, in which he acted as a consultant to Guinand and Benacerraf. The *Revista del Banco Obrero* journal is published. Villanueva gives a conference at MIT in Cambridge, Massachusetts, and is named corresponding member of the Academy of Architecture in France.

Fernández del Amo builds the Vega-viana Settlement in Cáceres, Spain. Bill Haley gives birth to rock and roll. Venezuelan bullfighter César Girón is the star figure of the Spanish season.

1955

The ninth Pan-American Congress of Architects is held at the University Campus of Caracas. Oscar Niemeyer visits Caracas.

The Banco Obrero begins work on the 2 de Diciembre estate, today called the 23 de Enero. After six months of work the first stage is inaugurated; the process will be repeated in 1956 and 1957 for the following stages. Within three years 9,000 apartments are erected to house more than 60,000 people, an unparalleled feat in all America. An exhibition of Calder's work is held in the Museum of Fine Arts in Caracas. Calder travels to Venezuela for the first and only time, and remains for a period of time to work in the workshop of the Industrial Technical School at the University Campus of Caracas, where he executes several works, among them the *Devil's Chair*, in tribute to Villanueva. Soto executes the *Cajita Villanueva*. Villanueva acquires a large number of the works from the kinetic and op art exhibition

The Bandung conference condemns colonialism. Juan Perón goes into exile. Sert designs Miró's Studio in Palma de Mallorca. Le Corbusier finishes the Chandigarh Supreme Court. Henry Russell Hitchcock organizes the *Latin American Architecture since 1945* exhibition at the Museum of Modern Art in New York.

Le *Mouvement* at the Denise Réné Gallery in Paris, with works by Alexander Calder, Marcel Duchamp, Jesús Soto, Jean Tinguely, and Victor Vasarély, among others. He becomes a member of the qualifying jury for the *International Painting Exhibition* in Valencia, Venezuela, and a corresponding member of the Brazilian Institute of Architects.

1956

The Banco Obrero begins work on ten developments, among them that of Simón Rodríguez, designed by Villanueva and Mijares. He is elected member of the Circle of Architectural Studies in Paris. He meets Walter Gropius in Cambridge.

Aalto designs the Vuoksenniska Church in Imatra, Finland. Eero Saarinen designs the TWA Terminal in New York.

1957

In spite of notable achievements in some areas, the government brutally crushes any attempt at democratization, generating discontent and opposition. Mass protest demonstrations are organized by the Patriotic Council.

Both the School of Architecture on the University Campus and the School of Petroleum Engineering in Maracaibo are inaugurated. The *Espacio y Forma* collection is founded, the first publication of the School of Architecture and Town Planning of the UCV. Villanueva executes the Chapel of La Asunción in the 23 de Enero development. Between 1957 and 1958 he designs and builds his Sotavento house in Caraballeda. On June 27 he gives a conference on "The Integration of the Arts" in the auditorium of the School of Architecture. Together with Calder he receives an honorary mention for Aula Magna Hall at the fourth Biennial of Sao Paolo, Brazil. An exhibition at the World Affairs Center in New York on Venezuelan architecture is sponsored by the Creole Petroleum Corporation and the Venezuelan Society of Architects. Luis Ramírez organizes it, Paolo Gasparini participates

The European Community is created. Nikita Khrushchev rises to power in the U.S.S.R. Lucio Costa plans Brasilia. Louis I. Kahn designs the Richards Medical Laboratories in Philadelphia; De la Sota designs the Civil Government Building in Tarragona. Jacobsen designs the Christensen Factory in Aalborg, Denmark. Sputnik is launched. Ingmar Bergman directs *Wild Strawberries*.

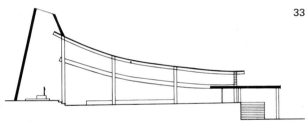

with photographic material for the panels, and Richard Neutra and Villanueva contribute written articles for the catalog. Villanueva becomes resident of the board of directors of the Venezuelan-French Cultural Institute.

1958

Pérez Jiménez is overthrown and a provisional junta is set up to prepare democratic elections. The First National Architects' Convention takes place. The first issue of *Revista de la Sociedad Venezolana de Arquitectos* is published.

Between 1958 and 1959 he draws up the designs to complete the sports area of the University Campus. One of these, the Covered Gymnasium, remains unfinished and a provisional roof is put in place. He delivers conferences at the School of Architecture and Town Planning in Buenos Aires and at the Brazilian Institute of Architects in Sao Paolo. He attends the talks on new cities organized in Rio de Janeiro by the Brazilian Institute for Education, Science, and Culture, the Brazilian Institute of Architects, and the UIA, sponsored by UNESCO. The Museum of Modern Art New York's 1955 exhibition *Latin American Architecture* is held at the School of Architecture of the Central University of Venezuela (UCV).

Charles de Gaulle is elected president of France. John XXIII becomes Pope. NASA is founded. Pacifism spreads. Oscar Niemeyer designs several buildings in Brasilia. Eladio Dieste designs the Atalántida Church in Uruguay.

1959

Rómulo Betancourt, president-elect of the republic, defends it against the supporters of the dictatorship and left-wing guerrillas. Saudi Arabia, Iraq, Kuwait, and Venezuela found OPEC, the Organization of Petroleum Exporting Countries. The new democratic constitution is approved.

Villanueva is elected honorary corresponding member of the Royal Institute of British Architects (RIBA) in London. In September he visits Le Corbusier in his atelier. A Vasarély exhibition is held at the Museum of Fine Arts of Caracas.

Fidel Castro assumes power in Cuba. Wright dies.

1960

Alexander Calder executes the work *The City*, which is acquired by the Museum of Fine Arts of Caracas. An exhibition of small mobiles, gouaches, and drawings is held in the same museum.

John F. Kennedy becomes president of the United States. The birth control pill is put on the market.

There are 1,400,000 inhabitants in the Caracas metropolitan area.

The Center for Historical and Aesthetic Research of the School of Architecture and Town Planning (FAU) of the Central University of Caracas is created.

1961

He lectures on the University Campus of Caracas at the Society of Architects in Paris. He receives an honorary doctorate from the Central University of Venezuela. He becomes member of the National Institute for Architectural Education in the United States, and the Commission of the Practice of the Profession of the International Union of Architects.

1962

He participates in the sixth congress of the International Union of Architects in London, with a paper on "The Influence of Concrete and of the Technical and Scientific Progress of Architecture Today and Tomorrow." He also participates in the Union of the Arts' "History of an Epoch 1890–1962" round table at Royaumont Abbey in France with a paper on "The Synthesis of the Arts: Southern Europe and Latin America". In November he meets Le Corbusier at his atelier, visits La Tourette and congratulates him by letter on his accomplishment.

1963

Between 1963 and 1967, together with Gorka Dorronsoro and Posani, he designs the School of Sanitary Engineering and the School of Economics, which will be finished in 1980, and the Schools of Industrial Engineering, Sciences, and Law, which are never built. He receives the National Prize for the University Campus of Caracas, awarded for the first time by the Venezuelan government. He participates

The Berlin Wall is erected. The Cold War intensifies. Gio Ponti and Pier Luigi Nervi design the Pirelli Building in Milan. Yuri Gagarin becomes the first person to travel in space.

Amnesty International is founded. The U.S. Telstar telecommunications satellite is launched. Mies van der Rohe designs the New National Gallery in Berlin, Robert Venturi the Vanna Venturi House in Philadelphia.

Kennedy is assassinated. Martin Luther King Jr. leads a civil rights march in Washington. Pope John XXIII dies. Hans Scharoun designs the Philharmonic Concert Hall in Berlin. James Stirling

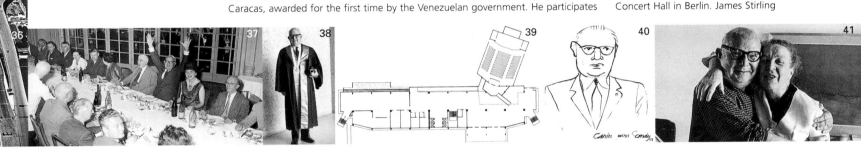

in the *Du paysage a l'expression plastique* exhibition in the House of Culture in Le Havre in France. He gives three conferences in the Museum of Fine Arts in Caracas about architecture, its current trends, and the city. He is president of the Organizing Committee of the First Congress of Bolivarian Architects. He becomes a member of the qualifying jury in the design competition for the Venezuelan Pavilion at the New York World's Fair.

1964

He gives a series of conferences in the United States: at the Pratt Institute in Brooklyn, New York; at the University of North Carolina in Raleigh, North Carolina; at the School of Architecture and Planning of MIT in Cambridge, Massachusetts; at the University of Pennsylvania in Philadelphia; and at the University of Virginia in Charlottesville. He participates in the American Institute of Architects' exhibition *Churches and Temples since the Post-war* in New York. He is honorary member of the Society of Colombian Architects. He receives the Golden Plaque from the Venezuelan Society of Architects and a diploma of recognition and tribute for his town planning work carried out in Venezuela. Sibyl Moholy-Nagy's book *Carlos Raúl Villanueva and the Architecture of Venezuela* is published in a bilingual English-Spanish edition in Venezuela and in English-German in Germany. The journal *Boletín del Centro de Investigación Históricas y Estéticas* is published and includes an essay by Villanueva on "The City and its History."

designs the Engineering Department at Leicester University, England. The Kodak Instamatic camera is invented. Heinrich Böll publishes *The Clown*.

Raúl Leoni is elected president. Buckminster Fuller visits Venezuela.

Sert designs Peabody Terrace residence hall for married students at Harvard University; Kahn designs the Salk Institute in La Jolla, California. King receives the Nobel Prize for Peace. Jean-Paul Sartre rejects the Nobel Prize for Literature. Mary Quant designs the miniskirt. Pop art succeeds at the Venice Biennial. The Beatles achieve worldwide fame.

Gorka Dorronsoro builds the villa in Cumbres de Curumo, Caracas. The Venezuelan Chamber of Architects is founded.

T. J. Sanabria builds the Central Bank of Venezuela, Caracas. M. Breto builds the El Camarón building, Caracas.

1965

He attends the *Current Architecture in America* exhibition in Madrid and gives a lecture entitled "Some Observations on the Current Development of Latin American Architecture" at the Institute of Hispanic Culture. He also gives a conference at the Mendoza Foundation in Caracas and sends two papers to the ninth Pan-American Congress of Architects held in Washington, which he is unable to attend: "Housing" and "The Development and Condition of the Cities of the Americas." He receives the diploma of merit from the Caracas City Council.

1966

He is a member of the jury of the third American Art Biennial held in Córdoba, Argentina, together with Alfred Barr, Arnold Bode, Sam Hunter, and Aldo Pellegrini. He meets his friend Amancio Williams. Villanueva receives the Mendoza Foundation's Prize for Sculpture for his work *Pic-nic*, made with scrap materials, in the fifth Salon of the Venezuelan Society of Architects. He is honorary president of the Venezuelan Society of Architects. On the occasion of the upcoming 400th anniversary of Caracas he publishes *Caracas en Tres Tiempos*. He receives the Order of José María Vargas, First Class, awarded by the Board of the Central University of Venezuela. He participates on the committee of consultant architects for the design of the Headquarters of the Bureau International de Travail (OIT) in Geneva.

Le Corbusier dies. Peter Collins publishes *Changing Ideals in Modern Architecture.*

Mao Tse-tung initiates the Cultural Revolution in China. Stirling designs the History Department at Cambridge University. Philips develops the cassette. Minimalist art is exhibited for the first time in museums. Alberto Giacometti dies.

1967

Villanueva builds the Venezuelan Pavilion for the Universal Exposition in Montreal. He attends the International Seminar on the Situation of the Historiography of Latin American Architecture in Caracas. He receives tribute from the American Academy of Design in Dallas, Texas. He becomes an honorary member of the Society of Bolivarian Architects. He is the recipient of the Order of the City of Caracas, awarded by the Caracas City Council, and of an honorary mention in the Municipal Prize for Architecture.

1968

The Monte Avila publishing house edits Walter Gropius's *Apollo in Democracy*, with a prologue by Villanueva. He attends the 12th Congress of Pan-American Architects in Bogotá. He is honorary member of the Colombian Cultural Center in Venezuela. He is the commissioner for the Venezuelan Stand at the 34th Venice Biennial, in charge of the assembly of the works designed by Marisol Escobar, the Venezuelan representative. He receives the Good Citizen Medal, awarded by the Pro-Venezuelan Society.

1969

He executes the draft designs of the Student Residence on the Paris University campus for the Fina Gómez Foundation, which publishes *Caracas a través de su Arquitectura* by Gasparini and Posani. The Student Assembly elects him representative of the School of Architecture and Town Planning (FAU). He receives the Latin

For the first time in Venezuela's history, a president hands power over to a candidate of the victorious opposition after free elections; the Christian Democrat Rafael Caldera (COPEI) becomes president at a moment when the rebel movements have been defeated and the majority of their leaders have been integrated into democratic political activity. A Calder exhibition is held in the Sala Mendoza, Caracas.

The Six Day War takes place between Israel and Egypt, Jordan, and Syria. R. Buckminster Fuller designs the U.S. Pavilion for Expo 67 in Montreal. Gabriel García Márquez writes *One Hundred Years of Solitude.*

Student protests in Paris and demonstrations against the Vietnam War in the United States. Martin Luther King is assassinated. Soviet tanks crush the reform movement in the Czech Republic.

250.000 people demonstrate against the Vietnam War. Aldo Rossi designs the Gallaterese apartment building in Milan. Neil Armstrong is the first man

American Prize of the Institute for the Promotion of Science, Art, and Design in Santa Fe, Argentina. He is named honorary member of the Mexican Society of Architects and corresponding honorary member of the La Salle Foundation of Natural Sciences of Venezuela.

1970

The OPEC Conference in Caracas establishes that 55 percent of the price of oil goes to the state of the producing country. A new phase of modernization begins on the basis of oil revenue.

He begins the design of the Jesús Soto Museum in Ciudad Bolívar, the last building he constructed. He participates as a panelist in the 13th Congress of Pan-American Architects in Puerto Rico, where he meets Sibyl Moholy-Nagy for the last time. Both Villanueva and Posani are invited to the Inaugural Seminar of the School of Architecture of the University of Los Andes, which names him honorary professor.

Salvador Allende is elected president of Chile. SOM designs the John Hancock Center in Chicago. In the United States, 50 percent of the female population works outside the home.

1971

The population of Venezuela is now 11 million; the population of metropolitan Caracas is 2.2 million.

The *Art in the Spaces of Man* exhibition is held in tribute to Villanueva at the Estudio Actual Gallery in Caracas; it then travels to the Center of Art and Communication in Buenos Aires. He is named honorary president of the Venezuelan Institute of Engineers.

Communist China is admitted in the United Nations. Sáenz de Oiza designs the Banco de Bilbao in Madrid.

1972

Building work begins on the second extension to the Museum of Fine Arts. The University of Los Andes in Merida awards him an honorary doctorate. His state of health begins to deteriorate rapidly, and he is admitted to the emergency ward of Merida hospital before being transferred to Caracas. The International Le Corbusier Association (AILC) elects him to join other key architectural figures in the Inter-

The Watergate scandal is exposed. The United Kingdom, Ireland, and Denmark join the European Community. Jorn Utzon designs the National Assembly Building in Kuwait. The Moscow Plan is drawn up.

national Committee of support for the association. The *Espacio y Forma* collection publishes Villanueva's drawings. The magazine *Punto* organizes an international competition of articles on Villanueva's architecture and an analysis of his work: the first prize is won by Makoto Suzuki. Villanueva is made honorary member of the Venezuelan Society of Town Planners.

1973

The Museum of Fine Arts in Caracas holds an exhibition of works from Villanueva's art collection.

Because of failing health he retires as professor of the School of Architecture and Town Planning of the UCV, where he had done a great deal of teaching with a group of young professors and students who referred to him affectionately as "Maestro Villanueva." He leaves an extensive and invaluable manuscript from his long and pioneering work in the training of architects, full of sketches and drawings: the *Apuntes Docentes*. The Jesús Soto Museum of Modern Art is inaugurated in Ciudad Bolívar, as is the second extension to the Museum of Fine Arts. Villanueva, who is now in a wheelchair and permanently disabled by his illness, lives long enough to see work progressing on the still-unfinished building.

OPEC's oil embargo causes a worldwide energy crisis, as a result of which oil consumption drops dramatically. A military coup overthrows Allende in Chile. I. M. Pei designs the Hancock Tower in Boston. Charles Jencks publishes *Modern Movements in Architecture*. The United States launches Skylab. Pablo Picasso and John Ford die.

1974

Carlos A. Pérez presides over the largest economic growth period in the history of Venezuela and nationalizes the main industries, iron and petroleum.

He receives the Homage of the Central University of Venezuela, the Banco Obrero, and the Chamber of Architects. Two plaques are unveiled that christen the Covered Plaza of the University Campus and Block 1 of El Silencio with his name.

Richard Nixon resigns presidency as a result of the Watergate scandal.

1975

Carlos Raúl Villanueva dies on August 16 in Caracas.

The Vietnam War ends.

Postscript

1976: The Museum of Fine Arts of Caracas holds an exhibition on the life and work of Villanueva. **1978:** *Arquitecturas de Villanueva* by Posani is published. **1980:** The building that was the headquarters of the Banco Obrero and Banco Agrícola y Pecuario, and which was remodeled by Villanueva in 1929, is declared a National Historical Monument. **1982:** An exhibition of Villanueva's drawings and sketches is held at the National Art Gallery in Caracas. **1987:** Several important anniversaries are celebrated: 50 years of the Venezuelan Pavilion at the International Exposition in Paris; 30 years of the School of Architecture and Town Planning and of the Sotavento house; and 20 years of the Venezuelan Pavilion at the Montreal Expo. **1988:** Between November 1988 and the end of February 1989 the exhibition *Villanueva, the Architect*, held in the Museum of Contemporary Art in Caracas and organized by Maciá Pintó, Paulina Villanueva, and Pedro Sanz, offers a complete profile of Villanueva, his collection of art, and his architectural and town planning work. **1991:** There is an exhibition on Villanueva at the fourth Art Biennial of Havana, showing his work together with that of Luis Barragán from Mexico, Vilanova Artigas from Brazil, and Walter Betancourt from Cuba. **1992:** From December 1991 to February 1992, under the curatorship of María Elena Ramos and Olga Römer, the exhibition *Space: The Exhibition Space of a Museum, the Grammar of Space and the Other Image* is held, intended as an investigation into the space of the Caracas Museum of Fine Arts. **1993:** The exhibition *The Architecture of Carlos Raúl Villanueva* is held in the Fine Arts Circle of Madrid (International Conference on the Conservation of Historic Centers and Latin America's Architectural Heritage). The exhibition *Villanueva and the Soto Museum* is held in the Jesús Soto Museum in Ciudad Bolívar, on the occasion of its 20th anniversary. **1994:** The following are declared National Historic Monuments: the Bullring in Maracay; the Jardín Hotel building in the same city; the University Campus of Caracas; and the museums of Fine Arts and of Natural Sciences, also in Caracas. **1997:** The exhibition *Genesis of a Building: The Designs of the FAU* is organized by the Center of Information and Documentation of the School of Architecture and Town Planning of the Central University of Venezuela, on the occasion of the 40th anniversary of the faculty building. **1998:** The exhibition *At the End of the Century. One Hundred Years of Architecture*, organized by the Los Angeles Museum of Contemporary Art, travels to different countries until the year 2000. It includes several works by Villanueva. **1999:** The School of Architecture and Town Planning of the Central University of Venezuela, via the Information and Documentation Center, starts proceedings to have the University Campus of Caracas declared as part of the Heritage of Mankind by UNESCO. Villanueva posthumously receives the Gold Insignia of the City of Caracas and the Prize for Excellence awarded by the mayor's office of the Libertador Municipality, Federal District. **2000:** The 100th anniversary of Villanueva's birth, celebrated with a program that includes several publications and exhibitions to be held both in Venezuela and abroad, among them the exhibition organized by the Council of Andalusia and the Ministry of Public Works of Spain. This book is the official catalog of that exhibition.

1 Nineteenth-century colonial house in Caracas (demolished in 1953).
2 Colonial patio-house (current Colonial Museum), Caracas.
3 Villanueva, 1918.
4 Villanueva with his parents and brothers in Málaga, 1919.
5 One of the many streets of Caracas using a colonial typology still being built as late as the 1930s and 1940s.
6 Draft design for a club in Costa Rica, 1927.
7 The architect working in Maracay, 1932.
8 Villanueva next to Juan Bernardo Arismendi, Pimpa Arismendi de Ugueto, and Margot, his wife, 1933.
9 Plaza Bolívar and Jardín Hotel, Maracay, 1929–30.
10 Villanueva on the terrace of his first house in La Florida, 1934.
11 Villanueva with Luis Malaussena and others during the construction of the Venezuelan Pavilion in Paris, 1937.
12 Maurice Rotival Plan for Caracas.
13 Plaza La Concordia, Caracas, 1940.
14 Villanueva during the redevelopment of El Silencio, 1944–45.
15 Aerial view of Caracas, with the Simón Bolívar Towers in the foreground and the 23 de Enero estate in the background.
16 Francisco de Miranda Cooperative Housing Estate, Caracas, 1948.
17 Construction of the Coronel Delgado Chalbaud Neighborhood Unit, Caracas, 1948–50.
18 Dedication by Auguste Perret, 1948.
19 Villanueva and José Luis Sert visiting the University Campus under construction, 1951.
20 Dedication by Alexander Calder when he met Villanueva, 1951.
21 Villanueva, Wright, and Neutra, among others, during the Pan-American Congress of Architects held in Mexico, 1952.
22 Villanueva in Paris, during the tribute paid to him by his former atélier fellows, 1952.
23 Villanueva with Henri Laurens and Antoine Pevsner in Fernand Léger's studio, 1953.
24 TABO working group, 1953.
25 Villanueva and Mateo Manaure in the University Campus, 1953.
26 Tenth Inter-American Conference at the Aula Magna Hall, February 1954.
27 Villanueva with the architect Guido Bermúdez at the TABO, 1954.
28 Villanueva, Victor Vasarély, and Jesús Soto in Paris, 1955.
29 Catalog cover dedicated to Margot Villanueva, 1955.
30 Villanueva next to Alexander Calder and Alejandro Otero at the Museum of Fine Arts, 1955.
31 La Rinconada Racetrack in the 1950s.
32 Alexander Calder and Villanueva next to *Devil's Chair*, 1955.
33 Section of the Church for the University Campus, Caracas, 1955 (not executed).
34 Villanueva with Richard Neutra at the University Campus, 1958.
35 Villanueva with Le Corbusier and Claudius Petit in Paris, 1959.
36 Highway articulating Caracas in the 1960s.
37 Villanueva with his fellow students at the Hotel Lutetia in Paris, 1960.
38 Villanueva receiving an honorary doctorate at the Central University of Venezuela, 1961.
39 Plan of the School of Economics, University Campus of Caracas, 1963–67.
40 Portrait of Villanueva drawn by Calder in 1963.
41 Villanueva with Sibyl Moholy-Nagy, 1964.
42 School of Sanitary Engineering, University Campus of Caracas, 1963–67.
43 Villanueva giving a lecture in Madrid, 1965.
44 The architect during a trip to Italy in 1966.
45 Villanueva in Geneva, with the Committee of Architects for the Headquarters of the OIT, 1966.
46 George Kubler and Villanueva in the Aula Magna Hall, 1967.
47 Alfredo Boulton's house in Margarita, with Leonardo Benévolo and Juan Pedro Posani, among others, 1967.
48 Villanueva with Jesús Soto, Ricardo de Sola, and Arthur Erickson in Montreal, 1967.
49 Villanueva at the reception ceremony of the American Academy of Design in Dallas, 1967.
50 Sketch for the assembly of Marisol Escobar's work at the Venice Biennial, 1968.
51 Villanueva with Amancio Williams in Argentina, 1969.
52 In the auditorium of the School of Architecture during the Renewal Movement, 1969.
53 Jesús Soto and Villanueva in Caoma, 1970.

bibliography

Abbreviations used in this bibliography

CONAC Consejo Nacional de Cultura
   (National Cultural Council of Venezuela)
FAU Facultad de Arquitectura y Urbanismo
   (School of Architecture and Urbanism)
UCV Universidad Central de Venezuela
   (Central University of Venezuela)
ULA Universidad de Los Andes
   (Los Andes University)

Villanueva texts and materials published in books and other publications

La Caracas de Ayer y de Hoy. Su Arquitectura Colonial, la Reurbanización de El Silencio. Paris: Draeger Frères Imprimeurs, 1950.

"Algunas Observaciones sobre el Desarrollo Actual de la Arquitectura Iberoamericana." Brochure. Caracas: Imprenta Nacional, 1958, p. 8.

"Presentación" by Gasparini, Graziano. In *Templos Coloniales de Venezuela.* Caracas: Italgráfica, 1959.

La Integración de las Artes, no. 3 Colección Espacio y Forma. Caracas: FAU-UCV, 1960, p. 12.

Escritos, no. 13 Colección Espacio y Forma. Caracas: FAU-UCV, 1965, p. 49.

"Alvar Aalto," in *Arquitectura de Finlandia.* Catalog. Caracas: FAU-UCV/Finnish Museum of Architecture, 1966.

Caracas en Tres Tiempos. Caracas: Ediciones de la Comisión de Asuntos Culturales del Cuatricentenario de Caracas, 1966, p. 208.

"Prólogo" by Gropius, Walter. In *Apolo en la Democracia.* Caracas: Monte Avila Editores, 1968, pp. 9–11.

Dibujos de Carlos Raúl Villanueva, no. 16 Colección Espacio y Forma. Caracas: FAU-UCV, 1972, p. 62.

Textos Escogidos. Caracas: Centro de Información y Documentación de la FAU-UCV, 1980, p. 101.

Caracas en Tres Tiempos. Caracas: Ediciones de la Dirección de Información y RR.PP. de la Gobernación del Distrito Federal, 1983, p. 222.

La Vivienda Popular en Venezuela 1928–1952. Caracas: Banco Obrero, undated, p. 140.

Los Bocetos de la FAU. Serie Bocetos, Cuadernos de la FAU-UCV Caracas: Centro de Información y Documentación de la FAU-UCV, 1997.

Síntesis de las Artes. Serie Bocetos, Cuadernos de la FAU-UCV. Caracas: Centro de Información y Documetación de la FAU-UCV, 1998.

Villanueva texts published in journals

"Proyecto Tema 'S.O.S.' Proyecto presentado en el Concurso para el Colegio de Ingenieros de Venezuela." *Revista del Colegio de Ingenieros de Venezuela*, no. 135 (April/May/June 1940), pp. 546–47.

"El Sentido de Nuestra Arquitectura Colonial." *Revista Shell*, no. 3 (June 1952), pp. 16–22.

"La vie artistique à Paris telle que nous l'a racontée Carlos Raúl Villanueva." *Compás* (Institute Culturel Venezuelien-Français, Caracas; January 1955), p. 17.

"La Enseñanza de la Arquitectura. Respuesta a un Cuestionario." *Integral*, no. 6 (February 1957).

"Las Experiencias de un Ensayo de Integración: la Facultad de Arquitectura y Urbanismo." *A. Hombre y Expresión*, no. 4 (July 1957), pp. 6–19.

"La Integración de las Artes." *Integral*, no. 13 (November 1958).

"Creación de Ciudades y Leyes de Indias." *El Farol*, no. 192 (January/February 1961), pp. 5–12.

"El Arquitecto." *Punto*, no. 2 (March 1961).

"Arquitectura Colonial." *Punto*, no. 3 (July 1961).

"Nuestras Ciudades de Ayer y de Hoy." *Revista del Colegio de Ingenieros de Venezuela*, no. 292 (July/September 1961), pp. 38–53.

"Influencias del Concreto y del Progreso Técnico y Científico en la Arquitectura de Hoy y Mañana." Speech delivered at the sixth Congress of the International Architects Union, *Punto*, no. 4, FAU-UCV, Caracas, November 1961.

"Reflexiones Personales." *Punto*, no. 7 (May 1962).

"Un Compañero que se va: Carlos Guinand." *SVA*, Bulletin of the Sociedad Venezolana de Arquitectos, no. 11 (May/June 1963), pp. 7–11.

"Síntesis de la Artes." *Punto*, no. 13 (July 1963).

"La Ciudad." *Punto*, no. 14 (September 1963).

"La Arquitectura Francesa." *Punto*, no. 15 (November 1963).

"Un Compañero que se Va: Carlos Guinand." In *Homenaje a Carlos Guinand*, no. 12 Colección Espacio y Forma (1964), pp. 7–11.

"El Desarrollo y Condición Presente de las Ciudades de las Américas." Speech delivered at the 11th Pan-American Congress of Architects, Washington, June 1965. Published in *Punto*, no. 24 (July/August 1965), pp. 13–15.

"La Vivienda." Speech delivered at the 11th Pan-American Congress of Architects, Washington, June 1965. Published in *Punto*, no. 24 (July/August 1965), pp. 16–17.

"Luminosa Trayectoria: Le Corbusier." *Punto*, no. 25 (November/December 1965), p. 7.

"Desarrollo de la Arquitectura Iberoamericana." Speech delivered in Madrid on December 10, 1965. Published in *Punto*, no. 26 (January/February 1966), pp. 12–17.

"Alvar Aalto." *Punto*, no. 26 (January/February 1966), p. 25.

"La Ciudad de Hoy." *Excelsior*, Mexico City (24 December 1967).

"Gropius." *Punto*, no. 39 (September 1969), pp. 17–19.

"Mensaje a los Estudiantes." *Punto*, no. 46 (June 1972), p. 7.

"La Arquitectura, sus Razones de Ser, las Líneas de su Desarrollo." Conference (1) delivered at the Museum of Fine Arts of Caracas, 28 May 1963. Published in *Punto*, no. 46 (June 1972), pp. 179–83.

"Tendencias Actuales de la Arquitectura." Conference (2) delivered at the Museum of Fine Arts of Caracas, 13 June 1963. Published in *Punto*, no. 46 (June 1972), pp. 184–89.

"La Ciudad del Presente, del Pasado y del Porvenir." Conference (3) delivered at the Museum of Fine Arts of Caracas, 2 July 1963. Published in *Punto*, no. 46 (June 1972), pp. 189–93.

"Síntesis de las Artes." *Revista del Colegio de Ingenieros de Venezuela*, no. 294 (October 1972), pp. 8–13.

"La Ciudad." *Revista del Colegio de Ingenieros de Venezuela*, no. 313 (March 1979), pp. 5–11.

"Apuntes Docentes." *Punto*, no. 64 (October 1982), pp. 106-11.

"Apuntes Docentes." *Punto*, no. 65 (1983), pp. 138–43.

Texts on Villanueva published in books

Anonymous. *Les concours d'architecture de l'année scolaire 1923–1924.* Quinzième année, Ecole Nationale Supérieure des Beaux-Arts. Paris: Auguste Vincent, 1924.

—. *Carlos Raúl Villanueva.* Catalog. Caracas: Banco Obrero, 1951.

—. "1951–1955 Plan Nacional de Vivienda." Brochure. Caracas: Banco Obrero, 1951.

—. "A Great Architect, Carlos Raúl Villanueva." In *Colombia and Venezuela, and the Guianas, Life World Library.* New York: Time Inc., 1956, pp. 114–15.

—. "Instituto de la Ciudad Universitaria." Brochure. Caracas: Editora Grafos, 1958.

—. "Carlos Raúl Villanueva." In the III Bienal Americana de Arte catalog. Córdoba, Argentina: Publicaciones IKA, 1966.

—. *Carlos Raúl Villanueva 1990–1975. Obra Gráfica* en la Colección Permanente de la Galería de Arte Nacional. Catalog. Caracas: Galería de Arte Nacional, 1982.

—. "Carlos Raúl Villanueva. Las Colecciones Privadas." In *Venezuela*, no. 7, Catalog. Caracas: Museo de Bellas Artes, undated.

—. "Ciudad Universitaria de Caracas." Brochure. Caracas: Cromotip C.A., undated, p. 8.

—. *IV Bienal de la Habana 1991.* Catalog. Havana: Centro Wifredo Lam, 1991, pp. 269–70.

Arroyo, Miguel. "La Ciudad Universitaria y el Proyecto de Integración de las Artes." In *Obras de Arte de la Ciudad Universitaria de Caracas,* Caracas, UCV/Monte Avila Editores/CONAC, 1991.

Bayon, D., and P. Gasparini. "Carlos Raúl Villanueva." In *Panorámica de la Arquitectura Latinoamericana.* Interview. Barcelona: Blume-UNESCO, 1977, pp. 199–215.

Bullrich, F. "Carlos Raúl Villanueva." In *New Directions in Latin American Architecture.* New York: George Braziller, 1969, pp. 73–82.

—. *Nuevos Caminos de la Arquitectura Latinoamericana.* Barcelona: Blume, 1969.

Conescal. *Conjuntos Universitarios de América Latina.* Mexico 1972.

Cuadra, M. *Architektur in Lateinamerika.* Darmstadt: Heinz-Jürgen Häusser, 1990.

De Sola, R. *Reurbanización de El Silencio. Crónica.* Caracas: Fundación Villanueva-INAVI-Armitano, 1988.

Granados Valdes, A. "Carlos Raúl Villanueva 1900–1975." In *Artistas de América.* Edited by Antonio Granados Valdés. Madrid, 1993, pp. 94–107.

Hernandez De Lasala, S. *En Busca de lo Sublime, Villanueva y la Arquitectura de la Ciudad Universitaria de Caracas.* Doctoral thesis. Caracas: FAU-UCV, 1999.

Larrañaga, E. "La Ciudad Universitaria y el Pensamiento Arquitectónico en Venezuela." In *Obras de Arte de la Ciudad Universitaria de Caracas,* Caracas, UCV/Monte Avila Editores/CONAC, 1991.

—. "On Technology, Ontology and Representation: The Plaza Cubierta at Universidad Central de Venezuela." In A. Naudé Santos and Susan (eds.). *Making Environments:Technology and Design.* Proceedings of the 10th Annual ACSA Technology Conference. Association of Collegiate Schools of Architecture, 1992.

Martinez Olavarria, L. "Villanueva, el Urbanista." In *Desarrollo Urbano, Vivienda y Estado.* Caracas: Fondo Editorial Alemo, 1996, pp. 142–48.

Moholy-Nagy, S. *Villanueva und die Architektur Venezuelas.* Stuttgart: Verlag Gerd Hatje, 1964.

—. *Carlos Raúl Villanueva y la Arquitectura de Venezuela.* Caracas: Lectura, 1964.

Moncada, B. *Renovación Urbana de El Silencio.* Mérida: Facultad de Arquitectura-ULA, 1977, p. 77.

Peter, J. *The Oral History of Modern Architecture.* New York: Harry N. Abrams, 1994.

Polito, L. *Las Quintas de Manuel Mujica Millán y Carlos Raúl Villanueva. Alrededor de los Años 30.* Master's thesis. Caracas: FAU-UCV, 1996, p. 283.

Posani, J. P. "Carlos Raúl Villanueva." In *Caracas a Través de su Arquitectura.* Caracas: Fundación Fina Gómez, 1969, pp. 365–439.

—. *Arquitecturas de Villanueva.* Caracas: Cuadernos Lagoven, 1978, p. 35.

—. *The Architectural Works of Villanueva.* Caracas: Lagoven Booklets, 1985, p. 75.

—. "Síntesis e Integración." In *Obras de Arte de la Ciudad Universitaria de Caracas,* Caracas, UCV/Monte Avila Editores/CONAC, 1991.

Robles Piquer, E. (RAS). "Villanueva y su Caracas en Tres Tiempos." In *Así lo Vi Yo. Personajes Venezolanos.* Caracas: Monte Avila Editores, 1971, pp. 19–21.

Sanz, P. *Los Caracas: de la Ciudad Sanitaria a la Ciudad Vacacional.* Caracas: FAU-UCV, 1985, p. 102.

Obras de Arte de la Ciudad Universitaria de Caracas. Caracas: UCV/Monte Avila Editores/Consejo Nacional de la Cultura, 1991.

La Ciudad del Saber. Ciudad: Universidad y Utopía, 1293–1993. Fifth International Conference on Historic Centres and Ibero-American Architectural Heritage. Madrid: Colegio Oficial de Arquitectos de Madrid, 1995.

Suzuki, M., and J. P. Posani. *C. R. Villanueva.* Contemporary Architects Series. Tokyo: Bijutsu Shuppan-sha, 1970 (Japanese edition).

Vegas, A. *La Ciudad Universitaria. Documentos Relativos a su Estudio y Creación.* Caracas: Grafolit, 1947.

Villanueva, P., and P. Gasparini. *Villanueva en Tres Casas.* Photographs. Caracas: Fundación Villanueva, 1999.

Zawisza, L. "El Silencio: Arquitectura y Urbanismo." In *El Silencio y sus Alrededores.* Caracas: FUNDARTE, 1985, pp. 41–64.

Articles on Villanueva published in journals

Calzadilla, J. "La Ciudad Universitaria: un Ensayo de Integración de las Artes." *Punto,* no. 28 (August/September 1966), pp. 27–31.

Dorronsoro, G. E. "A Propósito del Homenaje al Dr. C.R. Villanueva." *Punto,* no. 46 (June 1972), p. 175.

Ferris, J. "Villanueva: Doctor Honoris Causa." *Punto,* no. 2 (March 1961).

Garcia-Pablos, R. "Análisis de la Obra Arquitectónica de C.R. Villanueva." *Punto,* no. 46 (June 1972), pp. 165–72.

Larrañaga, E. "Villanueva y la Invención del Trópico" in *Imagen,* no. 100-47 (CONAC, 1988).

Lopez, M. "La Arquitectura del '2 de Diciembre' (Urbanización 23 de Enero)." *Boletín del C.I.H.E,* no. 27 (December 1986), pp. 148–72.

Meneses, G. "Los Artistas Extranjeros de la Ciudad Universitaria de Caracas." *El Farol* (March/April 1957), pp. 2–8.

Moholy-Nagy, S. "Bauten unter tropischer Sonne. Zum Werk des Venezolanischen Architekten Villanueva." *Bauwelt,* no. 24 (1960), pp. 679–84.

—. "Villanueva and the Uses of Art." *Arts,* no. 34 (September 1960), pp. 46–51.

—. "La Obra Arquitectónica de Carlos R. Villanueva." *Punto,* no. 46 (June 1972), pp. 33–72.

Muiño Loureda, A. "Ciudad Universitaria de Caracas: una Síntesis de las Artes Plásticas." *Punto,* no. 11 (February 1962).

Navarro, L. "Pintura y Escultura en la Ciudad Universitaria de Caracas." *Revista Shell,* no. 41 (December 1961), pp. 21–28.

Niño Araque, W. "Villanueva: Una Lección de Creatividad Estética y Humana" in *Imagen,* no. 100-47 (CONAC, 1988).

Porro, R. "La Arquitectura de Villanueva." *Integral,* no. 13 (November 1958).

—. "La Arquitectura de Villanueva." *Punto,* no. 46, Caracas, FAU-UCV (June 1972), pp. 105–17.

Posani, J. P. "Aula Magna, Ciudad Universitaria." *Integral,* no. 9 (November 1957).

—. "Piscina de la Città Universitaria di Caracas." *L'Architettura* (July 1961), pp. 181–86.

—. "Villa in Venezuela sulla costa dei Caribi." *L'Architettura,* no. 52 (February 1960), pp. 686–89.

—. "Villanueva, Premio Nacional de Arquitectura." *SVA,* Bulletin of the Sociedad Venezolana de Arquitectos, no. 12 (July/August 1963), pp. 4–10.

—. "Expo 67, Villanueva, Soto." *Boletín del CIHE,* no. 8 (October 1967), pp. 57–88.

—. "Aula Magna." *Punto,* no. 46 (June 1972), p. 118.

—. "Acepto que..." *Punto,* no. 46 (June 1972), pp. 176–78.

Rothenstein, Sir John. "A City of All the Arts in Venezuela." *The Sunday Times,* London, 9 April 1961.

Suzuki, M. "El Concepto de Espacio Cubierto." *Punto,* no. 46 (June 1972), pp. 73–77.

Tello, J. "Villanueva, Creador de Espacios." *Viasar,* no. 1 (April/May 1976), pp. 32–35.

Tenreiro, O. "El Villanueva Nuestro" in *Imagen,* no. 100-47 (CONAC, 1988).

Vayssiere, B. "Carlos Raúl Villanueva." *Punto,* no. 46 (June 1972), p.78.

Zawisza, L. "La Ciudad Universitaria de Caracas." *Punto,* no. 59 (October 1977), pp. 1–79.

Zevi, B. "Carlos Raúl Villanueva. Il Petrolio Riveglia gli Architetti." *L'Espresso,* Roma, 15 November 1964, p. 23.

Villanueva works in journals

A. *Hombre y Expresión.* "La Casa de Carlos Raúl Villanueva." (September 1955).

Architectural Forum. "The Pharmacy Faculty Building at Caracas University City." (June 1963), p. 106.

—. "Three Cubes: The Venezuelan Pavilion at Expo 67." (September 1967), pp. 58–59.

Arquitecturas Bis. "Homenaje de Venezuela a Carlos Raúl Villanueva." No. 16 (November 1976), p. 6.

C.A.V. (Colegio de Arquitectos de Venezuela). "Pabellón de Venezuela–Expo 67 Montreal." No. 3 (September 1967).

Carta de Venezuela. "Pujanza y Estabilidad Simboliza el Pabellón de Venezuela." No. 114 (April 1967), pp. 8–9.

Construcciones y Dotaciones Educativas (F.E.D.E. bulletin). "Escuela Gran Colombia (Francisco Pimentel)." No. 14 (January/February 1984), pp. 10–11.

Domus. "La Casa di Villanueva" (April 1956), p. 17.

—. "Nuovi Quartieri a Caracas C. R. Villanueva." (April 1956), pp. 9–11.

Inmuebles. "Carlos Raúl Villanueva. El Hacedor de Dos Mundos." No. 12 (June 1993), pp. 108–10.

Integral. "Facultad de Humanidades. Ciudad Universitaria de Caracas. Arquitecto: C. R. Villanueva." No. 6 (February 1957).

—. "Comunidad '2 de Diciembre,' Primera Etapa, 1955, Arquitectos: C. R. Villanueva–J. M. Mijares–J. Hoffman–Carlos Brando." No. 7 (May 1957).

—. "Comunidad '2 de Diciembre' Segunda Etapa, 1956, Arquitectos: C. R. Villanueva–J. M. Mijares–José Hoffman." No. 7 (May 1957).

—. "Comunidad '2 de Diciembre,' Tercera Etapa, 1957, Arquitectos: C. R. Villanueva–J. M. Mijares." No. 7 (May 1957).

—. "Unidad Residencial 'El Paraíso,' Arquitectos: C. R. Villanueva–Carlos Celis Cepero–J. M. Mijares." No. 7 (May 1957).

—. "Unidad Vecinal 'Simón Rodríguez,' Arquitectos: C. R. Villanueva–J. M. Mijares." No. 7 (May 1957).

—. "Cerro Piloto. Arquitecto Consultor: C. R. Villanueva. Arquitectos: G. Bermúdez, C. Brando, J. Centellas." No. 7 (May 1957).

—. "Unidad Vecinal en Coro. Arquitectos: C. R. Villanueva–C. Celis Cepero." No. 7 (May 1957).

L'Architecture D'Aujourd'Hui. "Faculté d'Odontologie, Cité Universitaire." No. 94 (February 1961), pp. 102–3.

—. "Piscine olympique de la Cité Universitaire de Caracas." No. 105 (December 1962), p. xxiv.

Punto. "Tres Obras no Construidas del Arquitecto C. R. Villanueva: Edificio para Estudiantes en la Ciudad Internacional de Paris, Edificio Principal de la Zona Rental UCV, Ampliación del Museo de Bellas Artes." No. 40–41 (January–March 1970), pp. 104–10.

—. "Nuevo Edificio del Museo de Bellas Artes." No. 53 (December 1974), pp. 17–29.

Reference works

Benevolo, L. *Historia de la Arquitectura Moderna.* 7th ed. Barcelona: Gustavo Gili, 1994, pp.726–28, 764, 790, 792–94, 897, 1029.

Botello, O. *Maracay, Noticias del Viejo Valle.* Maracay: Ediciones Centauro, 1980.

Boulton, A. *Imágenes, Macanao Ediciones.* Milan, 1982.

Bullrich, F. *Arquitectura Latinoamericana 1930–1970.* Buenos Aires: Editorial Sudamericana, 1969.

—. *New Directions in Latin American Architecture.* New York: George Braziller, 1969.

Calder, A. *Autobiographie.* Paris: Maeght Editeur, 1972.

Castedo, L. *A History of Latin American Art and Architecture.* New York: Frederick A. Praeger, 1969.

Curtis, W. *Modern Architecture since 1900.* Revised ed. London: Phaidon, 1998, pp. 502–3.

Chueca Goitia, F. *Historia de la Arquitectura Occidental.* Tomo VI. El Siglo XX, las Fases Finales y España. Madrid: Editorial Dossat S.A., 1980.

Fleming, J., H. Honour, and N. Pevsner. *The Penguin Dictionary of Architecture.* 4th ed. London: Penguin Books, 1991.

Fletcher, Sir Banister. Dan Cruickshank, ed. *Sir Banister Fletcher's A History of Architecture.* 20th ed. London and Oxford: RIBA and The University of London/ Architectural Press, 1996, pp. 1540–43.

Frampton, K. *Historia Crítica de la Arquitectura Moderna.* Barcelona: Gustavo Gili, 1993.

Frampton, K., and Y. Futagawa. *Modern Architecture 1920–1945.* New York: Rizzoli, 1983.

Gasparini, G., and J. P. Posani. *Caracas a Través de su Arquitectura.* Caracas: Fundación Fina Gómez, 1969.

Goldberg, M. *Guía de Edificaciones Contemporáneas de Venezuela.* Caracas Parte 1. Caracas: Centro de Información y Documentación FAU-UCV, 1982.

Gutiérrez, R. *Arquitectura y Urbanismo en Latinoamérica.* Madrid: Cátedra, 1983.

Hitchcock, H. R. *Latin American Architecture since 1945.* New York: Museum of Modern Art, 1955.

Hofmann, W., and U. Kultermann. *Modern Architecture in Color.* New York: The Viking Press, 1971.

Jacobus, J. *Twentieth-Century Architecture: The Middle Years 1940–1965.* New York: Praeger, 1966.

Jencks, C. *Architecture 2000: The New Concepts of Architecture.* London: Studio Vista/Architectural Association, 1971.

Kulterman, U. *Arquitectura Contemporánea.* Barcelona: Gustavo Gili, 1958.

Lopez Rangel, R. I. *Arquitectura y Subdesarrollo en América Latina.* Mexico City: Universidad Autónoma de Puebla, 1975, p. 145.

Moreno, J. *Monumentos Históricos Nacionales.* Caracas: Instituto de Patrimonio Cultural, 1998.

Nazoa, A. *Caracas Física y Espiritual* Caracas: Concejo Municipal del Distrito Federal, 1977.

Niño Araque, W., et al. *1950. El Espíritu Moderno.* Catalog. Caracas: Fundación Corp Group, 1998.

Peruga, I. *Museo de Bellas Artes de Caracas. Cincuentenario. Una Historia.* Caracas: Museo de Bellas Artes, 1988.

Peter, J. *Masters of Modern Architecture.* New York: George Braziller, 1958.

Posani, C. *Apenas Ayer... 20 Años de Fotografía de L.F. Toro.* Caracas: Fundación Neuman, 1981.

Ragon, M. l. *Esthétique de l'Architecture Contemporaine.* Neuchatel: Editions du Griffon, 1968.

Ramos G., A. *12 Pintores 7 Críticos de Arte.* Caracas: Concejo Municipal del Distrito. Federal, 1976.

Several Authors. *50 Years of Civil Engineering, 1904–1954.* Denmark: Christiani & Nielsen, 1954.

—. *Encyclopedia of Modern Architecture.* London: Thames and Hudson, 1963.

—. *América Latina en su Arquitectura.* Mexico City: Siglo XXI Editores, 1975.

—. *Diccionario de Arquitectos. De la Antigüedad a Nuestros Días.* Barcelona: Gustavo Gili, 1981.

—. *La Vivienda Multifamiliar/Caracas 1940–1970.* Caracas: Instituto de Arquitectura Urbana, 1983.

—. *Cronología Latinoamericana y el Mundo. 900 a.C.–1985 d.C.* Caracas: Biblioteca Ayacucho, 1986.

—. *Diccionario de Historia de Venezuela.* Caracas: Fundación Polar, 1988.

—. *El Espacio.* Catalog. Caracas: Museo de Bellas Artes, 1991, pp. 7–72.

—. *Imágenes de la Universidad Central de Venezuela.* "Una Casa que es una Ciudad, que es un País." Caracas: Dirección de Información y Relaciones, UCV, 1997.

—. *At the End of the Century. One Hundred Years of Architecture.* Catalog. Los Angeles: The Museum of Contemporary Art, 1998, pp. 293–94.

Ugueto, P. *J. B. Arismendi.* Caracas: Editorial Arte, 1980.

—. *Carlos Raúl Villanueva, un Moderno en Sudamérica.* Catalog. Caracas: Fundación Galería de Arte Nacional, 1999.

Villanueva's studio in Caoma, 1971